DEC - - 2016

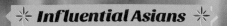
Influential Asians

MAYA LIN

Artist, Architect, and Environmentalist

Tricia Yearling

Enslow Publishing
101 W. 23rd Street
Suite 240
New York, NY 10011
USA

enslow.com

Published in 2017 by Enslow Publishing, LLC.
101 W. 23rd Street, Suite 240, New York, NY 10011

Library of Congress Cataloging-in-Publication Data
Names: Yearling, Tricia.
Title: Maya Lin : artist, architect, and environmentalist / Tricia Yearling.
Description: New York : Enslow Publishing, 2017 | Series: Influential Asians | Includes biblio
graphical references and index.
Identifiers: ISBN 9780766079007 (library bound)
Subjects: LCSH: Lin, Maya Ying--Juvenile literature. | Vietnam Veterans Memorial (Washing
ton, D.C.)--Juvenile literature. | Chinese American architects--Biography--Juvenile literature.
Classification: LCC NA737.L48 Y43 2017 | DDC 720.92--dc23

Printed in the United States of America

To Our Readers: We have done our best to make sure all websites in this book were
active and appropriate when we went to press. However, the author and the publisher
have no control over and assume no liability for the material available on those websites
or on any websites they may link to. Any comments or suggestions can be sent by e-mail to
customerservice@enslow.com.

Portions of this book appeared in the book *Maya Lin: Architect and Artist* by Mary Malone.

Photo Credits: Cover, p. 1 Glenn Koenig/Los Angeles Times via Getty Images; p. 4 Minehan
ullstein bild via Getty Images; p. 8 Maya Lin/Library of Congress/Wikimedia Commons/
MayaLinsubmission.jpg/public domain; p. 13 John Lamparski/Getty Images; p. 17 Steve
Northup/The LIFE Images Collection/Getty Images; p. 19 aceshot1/Shutterstock.com; p. 23
Richard Howard/The LIFE Images Collection/Getty Images; p. 26 Yale events and activities
photographs, 18522003(inclusive). Manuscripts & Archives, Yale University; p. 29 Lee Snider
Photo Images; p. 31 Jeff Malet Photography/Newscom; p. 34 Chip Somodevilla/Getty Images
p. 39 Harold Adler/Underwood Archives/Getty Images; pp. 43, 49, 87, 94 © AP Images; p.
47 Science Source/Getty Images; pp. 53, 77 Library of Congress; p. 60 John McDonnell/The
Washington Post via Getty Images; p. 63 Ethan K. San Francisco http://www.flickr.com/peo
ple/ethankan/Wikimedia Commons/Vietnam Memorial roses.jpg/CC BY-SA 2.0; p. 65 Joe
Raedle/Getty Images; p. 68 Harry Naltchayan/The Washington Post viaGetty Images; p. 70
G0T0/File:ThreeSoldiers2.JPG/Wikimedia Commons; p. 80 Markuskun at English Wikipe
dia/Wikimedia Commons The Civil Rights Memorial, Montgomery, AL.jpg/public domain;
p. 84 Thomas S. England/The LIFE Images Collection/Getty Images; p. 92 Jason Jones/Wiki
media Commons/Peace Chapel.jpg/public domain; p. 96 Andre Jenny/Alamy Stock Photo; p
99 Carol Highsmith/Library of Congress/Wikimedia Commons/Womens Table Highsmith.
jpg/public domain; p. 101 Glenn Koenig/Los Angeles Times via Getty Images; p. 103 Brad
Barket/Getty Images.

Contents

Maya Lin is an artist, architect, environmentalist, and activist.

Chapter 1

DEFINING MOMENTS

"**P**art of me is an artist. The other part builds architecture,"[1] says Maya Lin. Perhaps best known for designing the Vietnam Veteran's Memorial in Washington, DC, at the age of twenty-one, Lin's career as an artist and architect has flourished since its auspicious beginning. She has designed and created intimate studio artworks, large-scale memorials, buildings, and multimedia installations meant to raise awareness about biodiversity and habitat loss.

A committed environmentalist, Lin has used her diverse talents to address critical social and historical issues. "My work originates from a simple desire to make people aware of their surroundings and this can include not just the physical but the psychological world that we live in."[2]

Entry No. 1026

"Student wins war memorial contest!"[3] That was the news headlined in the newspapers on May 7, 1981. The competition for a design of a memorial to honor the veterans of the Vietnam War had been open to all citizens of the United States. But who expected a student to win?

Many architects, designers, and artists, known and unknown, had entered the contest. And the surprising winner over all other entrants was a twenty-one-year-old Chinese American student named Maya Ying Lin, who was in her senior year at Yale University.

Lin's submission was an unlikely choice for first place. Her design was described as somewhat smudged[4] and unprofessional looking. The first time he saw it, Jan Scruggs, the Vietnam War veteran who had conceived the memorial and the competition, said the design resembled a "big bat."[5] Other veterans wondered what it was about the design that had made such a strong impression on the judges.

Lin thought of herself as an artist first, and had only recently decided that she would make architecture her career. The winner of the competition would receive a prize of $20,000 and the likelihood of a permanent place in any national monument makers' Hall of Fame. Lin planned to use the money for further study in her chosen profession.

The group of Vietnam War veterans who sponsored the competition had recently formed a nonprofit corporation called the Vietnam Veterans Memorial Fund—VVMF. Their sole aim was to build a memorial in the nation's capital to the Vietnam War veterans. When the competition was announced in the fall of 1980, the VVMF received over five thousand inquiries about it.

By the deadline, March 31, 1981, more than fourteen hundred entries proposing mounds, statues, columns, and symbols of war had been submitted. The names of the creators were replaced with assigned numbers. The bulky packages containing the proposals, all submitted on two-by-four panels, were stored in an airplane hangar at Andrews Air Force base outside Washington. Set up for display, they covered over a mile of space. In late April, they were ready to be reviewed by the panel of judges, a group of eminent architects and landscape designers, who had one week to decide the winner.

The VVMF had hoped for a worthy memorial to come from the design competition. The only requirement for the memorial was that it had to feature the names of the nearly fifty-eight thousand American Vietnam War soldiers killed or missing in action. Other than that, the VVMF entrusted their project to the expert knowledge of the renowned panel of judges who knew what art was all about. Ideally, newspaper critic Wolf Von Eckardt said long before the competition was officially announced, that great monuments are "simply powerful ideas translated into a powerful response."[6] This was a prophetic statement, uncannily descriptive of the winning design.

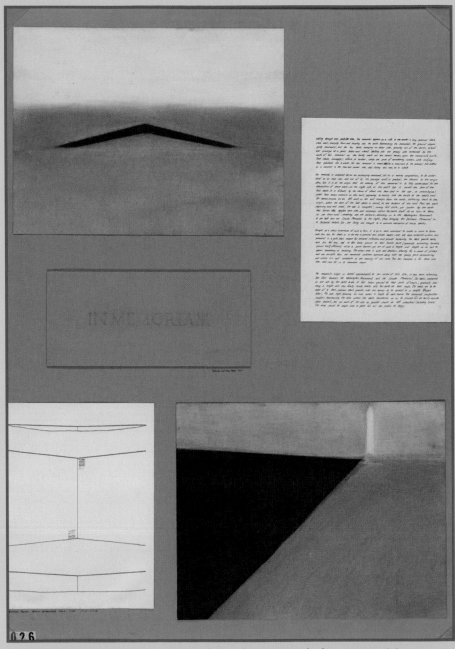

Lin submitted these plans when she entered the competition to design the Vietnam Veterans Memorial in Washington, DC.

The VVMF could have simply selected an architect and a design for the monument themselves. However, they believed an open competition would be both more democratic and more likely to increase public support for a memorial that commemorated veterans of a highly controversial and unpopular war. Their plan worked.

Although much of the public believed that holding a competition for a memorial design was something new, in fact such competitions had been held throughout American history. A competition in 1792 to determine the design of the presidential White House was won by Irish-born James Hoban for his classic, Grecian-inspired design. The design competition for the Washington Monument, another landmark in the nation's capital, was won by Robert Mills in 1833, although his design was later altered.

Maya Lin was following an honored American tradition by submitting, in open competition, her design for a national monument. What no one could predict was that the design of a young, Chinese-American student without any experience as an architect would turn out to be the "powerful idea" the judges were looking for.

A Clear Winner

The judges began their huge task by winnowing the field of 1,421 entries to thirty-nine designs, and then down to only eighteen. However, they kept returning to design No. 1026, which not only impressed them, but, they said, "haunted" them.[7]

Although the entry was not as polished as the designs by professional architects, it was strangely compelling. As the written description that accompanied the drawings explained, two long, black-marble walls carved with the names of the fifty-eight thousand soldiers killed or missing action in Vietnam would delve into the earth and then rise to meet at an angle. Together they would resemble two sides of a triangle.

Simple and direct though it was, the judges thought that entry No. 1026 elegantly fulfilled the requirements of the competition in a unique and powerful way. They noted the memorial's harmony with its location, which was the hallowed ground of Constitution Gardens on the Mall, near the Capitol. The memorial would be placed between the two of the greatest monuments in the city, the Lincoln Memorial to the west and the Washington Monument to the east.

At the end of the week, the judges voted. To be sure they agreed, they went back and voted again. There was no question—No. 1026 was unanimously selected for first place. "Of all the proposals submitted," the judges said, "this most clearly meets the spirit and formal requirements of the program. It is contemplative and reflective. It is superbly harmonious with its site."[8]

When it was revealed that the winning design was from an unconventional source, the news flashed across the country. Maya Lin became an immediate celebrity. She was interviewed, photographed, seen on television. Her life story—short as it was—was the subject of many

Maya Lin's Memorials

Although Maya Lin resists the label of being a builder of memorials, she has a total of five to her credit.

The Vietnam Veterans Memorial (Washington, DC, 1982)
In memory of the nearly fifty-eight thousand soldiers who died or were missing in action as a result of the Vietnam War

The Civil Rights Memorial (Montgomery, AL, 1989)
In memory of the events of the Civil Rights movement and the people who were killed during that time

The Women's Table (Yale University, New Haven, CT, 1993)
Memorial dedicated to the growing number of women of Yale University

Confluence Project (Art installations at several points along the Columbia River System in the states of Washington and Oregon, ongoing)
A tribute to the history, culture, and ecology of the native peoples of this region as affected by the Lewis and Clark Expedition

What Is Missing? (Several scientific institutions, website, and book, ongoing)
Memorial dedicated to raising awareness to the crises around the worldwide loss of habitat and its effects on biodiversity

newspaper articles. Praise and congratulations poured in, not only for the young designer, but for the VVMF too.

Maya Lin was described by B. Drummond Ayres in *The New York Times* as "pleased, enjoying herself."[9] When her design was made public, it was praised by many art critics. One said that the judges "must have felt a sense of excitement and discovery"[10] when they came upon Lin's design and selected it as the best of all the entries in the largest design competition ever held in the United States.

Expectations vs. Expertise

Enthusiasm for the design and the winner prevailed at the start. But as the end result of the competition received more publicity, stirrings of dissent arose over time. Many people, some of them prominent, disliked the design and protested its selection. Although it had been selected by a panel of highly trained experts, the design was unconventional and not what people expected.

It was quite a departure from the usual concept of a memorial—the Cenotaph in London, for example, a huge monument built to honor those (in this case, British soldiers killed in war) whose bodies were missing or buried elsewhere. In days gone by, when men wore hats, they raised them whenever they passed the Cenotaph.[11] Another famous traditional-style monument is at the back entrance to Arlington National Cemetery outside of Washington, DC. It is a sculpture of six United States marines raising the American flag on Iwo Jima during World War II.

Shown here at the 2015 MOCA Legacy Awards Gala, Maya Lin was thrust into the spotlight at a young age.

Many Vietnam War veterans across the country—those outside the Washington-based VVMF—were upset by the selection of Lin's design. They hadn't been consulted, and they were outraged by the fact that someone who knew nothing about the Vietnam War had designed a memorial for their comrades. This was a very emotional subject for them, as the war had been for the whole country.

A writer for *The Washington Post* commented that "a woman who was four years old when the first bodies came home, had designed a national memorial to be built on the Mall."[12] Other people found it ironic that an Asian-American woman had designed a memorial to an American military action in Southeast Asia.

However, the American public, on the whole, displayed no prejudice regarding that coincidence. Lin's family had left communist China to immigrate to the democratic United States, implying that ideology was more important to them than race.

The criticism turned into a controversy between those who praised the design as a fine example of modern art and those who preferred the older, more familiar style. After the elation of winning the competition, the pointed criticism about her design shocked Lin. "I will never know how much my age, my race, my gender played into the controversy."[13] As time went on, it changed her outlook. At the age of twenty-one, no longer sheltered in a college atmosphere, she was to learn a great deal—about people, politics, and compromises.

Chapter 2

ROOTS IN CHINA

Long before Maya Lin was born, her family lived in China. Her ancestors were wealthy, accomplished professionals. Both the Lins on her father's side and the Changs on her mother's side were successful doctors, lawyers, artists, and scholars. As part of an elite class, they joined the Nationalist party of Sun Yatsen, who was credited with overthrowing the last repressive Chinese dynasty in 1911. For more than a decade, China enjoyed a more open, democratic society.

In 1921, Lin Changmin, a lawyer and Maya Lin's grandfather, was sent by the Chinese government to Europe as director of his country's delegation to the League of Nations. Although that attempt by many nations to promote peace failed, it was eventually succeeded in 1946 by the present United Nations.

Mr. Lin's seventeen-year-old daughter, Lin Huiyin, accompanied her father.[1] She was a beautiful, intelligent young woman who made many friends, especially in London where she met well-known writers and poets. When the Lins returned to China, Hui-yin married, according to her father's wishes. The man she married was Liang Si-chang, an architectural historian.

The couple traveled to the United States to complete their education at the University of Pennsylvania. While in America, the young woman who would become Maya Lin's aunt enrolled for a term at Yale University, where she studied the architecture of stage design. Later, back in China, she and her husband traveled throughout the country, locating and saving many of China's old, historic buildings.

Maya's father, Henry Huan Lin, was the younger brother of Lin Huiyin. He has said that his daughter Maya resembles her. Like his sister, he said, "Maya is very emotional, very sensitive."[2] Henry Lin added that all the female Lins were strong, independent women. He himself was an artist in ceramics, and a collector of ancient porcelain pieces.

Political Change in China

Several years after Sun Yatsen's time, during the 1920s and 1930s, China was unsettled politically by warring factions. The Nationalists were opposed by an evergrowing Communist party, which was supported by the Soviet Union. Fighting continued during and after World War II.

Lin descends from an accomplished Chinese family. Their wealth allowed them to flee to the United States when the regime changed.

General Chiang Kaishek, who led the Nationalists, was defeated in 1949 and fled to the island of Taiwan, which had been occupied by Japan and ceded back to China by the Japanese after the war. There the Nationalists established the Republic of China in Taiwan.

Planting Seeds in the United States

Meanwhile, people in mainland China who had belonged to the Nationalist party were considered a danger to the new regime. Those who could afford to escaped from China during the late 1940s, and, like Maya Lin's parents, some of them came to the United States.

Because of his excellent educational qualifications, Maya's father, Henry, was able to obtain a position at Ohio University in Athens, Ohio. Maya's mother, Julia Chang, was the daughter of a physician. She had been accepted into Smith College in Northhampton, Massachusetts and awarded a scholarship. Her family smuggled her out of China on a fishing boat with nothing but her acceptance telegram and two ten-dollar bills sewn into the collar of her dress.[3]

Julia graduated from Smith in 1951 and soon after met Henry Lin. They were married and settled in Athens, Ohio, where both of them were on the faculty of Ohio University for many years. The Lins' two children were born in Athens, first a son, Tan, and three years later, Maya, on October 5, 1959. Her name came from the Hindu goddess, the mother of Buddha, but more personally, it was also the name of a friend of Julia Chang's at Smith College, "a beautiful Indian girl."[4]

Maya's Chinese middle name, Ying, can be translated as "precious stone."

At Ohio University, Julia Lin taught Oriental and English literature. She also wrote poetry and had books published on the subject of Chinese poetry. Henry Lin rose to the position of professor of art at the university and, in time, became dean of the department of fine arts.

Maya and her brother spent a lot of time on and around the university campus, which had a profound effect on them both. "I've been making art since I was— ever since I can remember," said Lin. "My dad was Dean of Fine Arts, and so my afterschool hours were spent in at the ceramics studio. Art has been second nature to me."[5]

Lin grew up in the college town of Athens, Ohio. Both of her parents were professors on the faculty of Ohio University and provided Maya with a love of the arts.

The college atmosphere of Athens, a town of some twenty-two thousand residents, characterized the area. Lin believed Athens was a "perfect" place to grow up. "You could leave your keys in your car, leave your door unlocked."[6]

Ideal as this life was, however, Maya Lin has admitted that she never felt really at home in Athens. "I grew up in the middle of the country, in Ohio. We were the only Chinese family growing up there, so I didn't have a community to be a part of."[7] In part, that was because her parents did not consider Athens their real home. "Their home was gone," Maya said.[8]

She and her brother, who were part of an extremely close-knit family, reflected their parents' feeling of being strangers in a strange land. But with their varied artistic talents, they were creatively occupied in a house cluttered with books and art materials. Art and literature were part of the Lins' daily life. Says Lin, "Growing up both Chinese and American in this country helped set up, maybe, an interest in—I call it the boundary line— the line between opposites, and I'm very drawn to that."[9]

Scholars, Poets, and Artists

The Lin children shared their parents' interests. Maya watched her father at his pottery wheel and as a small child was allowed to "throw" and fire pottery. As Tan grew up, his interest centered on poetry, and like his mother, he became a poet.

Maya spent a lot of time in her room, constructing little villages of paper or leftover materials from her

Museum of Chinese in America

Maya Lin was asked to reimagine the space in which New York City's Museum of Chinese in America (MOCA) was located to better "symbolize institutional growth from its roots as the local Chinatown History Project to its expanding identity as the country's preeminent National Chinese American history museum."[10]

The new 12,500-square-foot space opened in 2009, and brings 160 years of Chinese-American history to life through exhibitions, educational, and cultural programs. Lin felt so strongly about supporting MOCA's mission, she joined its board of directors.

father's studio. "I grew up, as a kid, making everything in my bedroom. And there is a side to me that is very much unwitting in my imagination. One could say that it's infinite and one could also say that it's slightly hermetic in feel at times."[11] As she grew older, she worked on ceramics, sculpture, and silversmithing.

In addition to art, Lin was drawn to nature and the environment. She enjoyed bird-watching and wandering in the woods near her home. That passion for the environment would motivate Lin later on, when she was designing buildings, other memorials, and individual pieces of art. She was always "siteoriented,"[12] as she said, in her consideration for keeping intact the natural setting of a planned structure.

Phil McCombs, a writer for *The Washington Post*, quotes from Lin Yutang, a well-known Chinese author (no relation to Maya Lin) who said, "The best architecture is that which loses itself in the natural landscape and becomes one with it, belongs to it."[13]

Both Lin and her brother preferred reading to watching television. As a child, Lin liked stories about dwarfs and elves and magical lands, such as *The Lion, the Witch and the Wardrobe* by C. S. Lewis and *The Hobbit* by J. R. R. Tolkien. Later on, she enjoyed the tales of Greek mythology. With her brother, she played chess and solved puzzles involving problems in logic. Photography was a strong interest for her.

The Lin children had freedom to pursue their own interests and control their own time. A strong sense of responsibility had been instilled early in the children. They studied and worked at their own pace. "My parents brought us up to decide what we wanted to do, where we wanted to study," Lin said. "They never forced us to do anything. We always had a choice."[14]

When she started high school, Lin found that her interests were not like those of most of her classmates. She said that "everyone was worried about getting A's, B's, and C's. I really thought it was kind of stupid. High school was really miserable. I disliked talking to people. Socially, I kind of ignored the whole scene. Boys and girls all taking themselves so seriously. The girls into makeup. It was just not at all my idea of a life, of anything interesting."[15]

Lin was more interested in figuring out a problem in trigonometry than in being one of the crowd. Although she has said, jokingly, "I guess you could say I was somewhat of a nerd,"[16] she also said frankly that she was not happy in high school.

Maya did, in some ways, appear to be a typical high school student. She dressed like all the others in school—jeans, T-shirts, and sneakers. She wore her hair long, hanging straight down her back. And, like many of her contemporaries, she worked at a local McDonald's. "It was the only way to earn some money," she said.[17]

Lin was an excellent student. Math was her favorite subject. She read books on a college level. She took some college courses while still in high school and was accepted by the college of her choice—Yale University

Maya Lin was a high achiever when it came to her studies. She excelled in most subjects but was not interested in the social aspects of high school life.

in New Haven, Connecticut. Her brother had decided to attend Columbia University in New York City. Lin chose Yale because, as she said, it was "academically challenging."[18]

Yale may very well have chosen her not only for her high academic standing— she was covaledictorian of her graduating class—but also for her artistic talent and her family background. Whatever it was that drew Maya Lin and Yale University together, it was a fortunate happening for both of them, as later events would prove.

Chapter 3

To Lin, Yale was "the first place where I felt comfortable,"[1] she said. "I'm a true-blue Yalie."[2] Lin's creativity as well as her love of learning were recognized early on by her teachers. She found the university atmosphere to be one where students and professors from all over the world came together. Even after graduation, Lin often returned to Yale.

As an undergraduate, Lin lived in a campus residence hall (dormitory) with a roommate, Liz Perry, who became a good friend. With other friends, Lin often went roller skating for relaxation. Her studies for the first two undergraduate years were focused on the liberal arts curriculum. She studied literature, philosophy, and science, among other subjects. Of the electives possible, Lin chose photography. She read a great deal and, like many other students, pondered the significance of life and death, the meaning of existence.

Lin thrived at Yale, taking advantage of all the university had to offer. In 1987, she received an honorary doctorate from her alma mater.

Although Lin was not quite the loner of her high school days, she often went on solitary walks through the streets of New Haven. Not long after she arrived at Yale, she discovered Grove Street cemetery, right in the heart of the city. She returned to it whenever she wanted to spend quiet time by herself. "There's something peaceful about it," she said. "You feel removed. You feel you're in their world . . . the world of the dead."[3]

Death to her then was still an abstract idea—something not real. She thought a lot about it, however, as she strolled through the cemetery. "I've always been intrigued with death," she explained, "and man's reaction to it."[4] She noted the ways the dead are remembered—the memorials, statues, epitaphs on the headstones. "Everybody knows I'm morbid,"[5] she said lightly, in explanation of her fascination with the subject. Her friends, however, would deny that she was morbid. They described her as "artistic, emotional, and sensitive."[6]

Major Decisions

After the general academic studies of their first two years, Yale students select a major, or a field on which they concentrate, for the remaining two years. In addition to its undergraduate college, Yale offers many schools of specialized advanced study, including medicine, law, drama, and architecture. Many students, after earning their bachelor's degree, enroll in the graduate school for their area of specialty to earn a master's degree.

Lin's decision to major in architecture was spontaneous. As she explains it, she was sitting in the college library one day, staring up at the ceiling, "at all the lines and painting on it…and suddenly, I decided I was going to be an architect. Just like that."[7]

Although it might appear to have been an impromptu decision, it really wasn't. All her life, Lin had been influenced by her family's artistic background. Her aunt, Lin Huiyin, was part of it. Her father was an artist, her mother a poet. Designing things—model towns, ceramics, sculptures—came from Lin's own interest in artistic creation. She considered herself an artist, and architecture was art on a large scale.

Study Abroad

In her junior year of college, Lin went with a group of other Yale students to Europe to study for a semester. She attended Copenhagen University in Denmark. Enrolled in courses in city planning and landscape design, she enjoyed walking around the section of Copenhagen known as Norrebro.

One of her assignments was to study that area, with its well-laid-out residential avenues and a beautiful, park-like cemetery. She noted that the cemetery was a place where people could go to enjoy the natural beauty of the surroundings. The locations of cemeteries in other European cities, such as Paris and London, impressed Lin in the same way. "European countries make their graveyards into living gardens,"[8] Lin said. People visited them to relax in the midst of teeming cities. On Sundays, parents might bring their children along to stroll and enjoy seeing the trees and flowers.

Many contemporary city planners consider cemeteries to be an essential "green space" for a balanced urban environment. Some of them include paths for jogging, biking, and hiking, as well as picnic and other recreational areas.

While in Denmark, Lin took trips to many famous sites and buildings in different European countries, the very old structures as well as the new. As an aspiring architect, she took the opportunity to see firsthand the architecture of the early Greeks, which in its classic, balanced proportions has influenced Western architecture for over two thousand years. She visited the buildings of the Acropolis in Athens, where the Parthenon—the

While at Yale, Lin often visited the historic Grove Street Cemetery to reflect on life and death. This photo shows the Egyptian-style monumental entrance gateway into the cemetery.

Capturing the Landscape

Lin's art, architecture, and memorials are all heavily influenced by appreciation for nature. Lin says, "My sculptures deal with naturally occurring phenomenon and they are embedded and very closely aligned with geology and landscape and natural Earth formation."[9]

"Folding the Chesapeake," which is at the Smithsonian American Art Museum in Washington, DC, recreates Baltimore's Chesapeake Bay in green marbles spread across the wooden floor , and white walls and ceiling of a room dedicated to the piece. "Seven Earth Mountain" features seven giant hills of dirt, which formed the backdrop for designer Philip Lim's 2015 spring fashion show. And "Storm King Wavefield" transforms a former gravel pit in Mountainville, New York, into an expanse of grassy, green, ocean-like waves.

ancient temple dedicated to the goddess Athena—stands. She saw the palace of Knossos on the island of Crete, a surviving reminder of the architecture of the Bronze Age of over four thousand years ago.

Lin also saw examples of modern architecture in Europe, buildings designed by two great architects of the modern style—Mies Van Der Rohe and Walter Gropius. Both of these famous men emigrated to the United States from Germany in the 1930s before the Nazis took control of their country. Their ideas greatly influenced the study of architecture in the American universities, especially Yale and Harvard.

Maya Lin's installation "Folding the Chesapeake" was first exhibited at The Renwick Gallery in Washington, DC. Lin used fiberglass marbles in a construction that suggests the Chesapeake Bay.

Lin was surprised to learn that ethnic differences in Denmark were not as acceptable as they were in the United States. One day when she boarded a streetcar and sat down, everybody near her rose and sat somewhere else.[10] For the first time, Lin became aware that her Asian appearance might disturb people.

The experience made her appreciate the United States and say later in an interview that although she could be identified as Chinese American, if she had to choose between the two, she would choose American. "I don't have an allegiance to any country but this one; it is my home . . . still a place where a lot can get done. This is a country that allows you the freedom to do what you can."[11] More than twenty years later, when talking about her work with the Museum of Chinese in America (MOCA), Lin would also say, "No matter where you come from, you bring it with you a little bit . . . your heritage, your cultural identity, resonate[s] and help[s] shape who we all are today." [12]

Lin returned to Yale ready to begin her final undergraduate year. She would turn twenty-one in October of 1980, and after that she would graduate. Who could have predicted that something many times more momentous than her graduation would occur in the coming year and change the course of her life?

Chapter 4

AN UNLIKELY SELECTION

After the pivotal experience of living in another country for her junior year abroad, Maya Lin was ready to get back to work. She was ready to use all that she had learned and taken in during her time in Europe in her architectures studies.

Lin's final architecture project at Yale was a special assignment given by her professor, Andrus Burr. It was a big challenge, and it was very real. Burr's assignment was to design a memorial for the recently announced Vietnam War veterans' monument competition.

A Sacrifice Ignored

Jan Scruggs was an eighteen-year-old from Bowie, Maryland, when he enlisted in the US Army. Not a year later, he shipped out to Vietnam, where he served as an infantryman in the controversial war. During his two tours of duty, he witnessed half of his company being killed. He was wounded himself and returned from Vietnam with shrapnel still in his legs.

Back home in Washington, DC, Scruggs was appalled by the hostile reaction of the public to the returning veterans. There were was no welcome home, no parades or public ceremonies honoring their sacrifices. Anger and bitterness over the United States' involvement in the conflict was transferred to the soldiers who had served in the unpopular war.

Scruggs was bothered most by the lack of recognition for the sacrifice so many of his fellow soldiers had made. After brooding about it for several years, he announced to his wife, "I'm going to build a memorial to all the guys who served in Vietnam. It'll have the name of everyone killed."[1]

Jan Scruggs believed that America needed such a memorial: recognition for the veterans, reconciliation for the people. He began his crusade alone. Very little attention was paid to his quest for contributions until a local television station gave him a small spot on its nightly news program. Scruggs's story attracted two prominent lawyers in Washington, also Vietnam veterans—John Wheeler and Robert Doubek. Together with Scruggs, they formed the nonprofit Vietnam Veterans Memorial Fund (VVMF) to carry on the fund drive, and from there the campaign took off.

Vietnam War veteran and president of the Vietnam Veterans Memorial Fund, Jan Scruggs speaks during a Memorial Day event at the Vietnam Veterans Memorial in Washington, DC.

The People Come Through

Through the tireless efforts of the VVMF leaders and its many volunteers, the number and size of the donations increased dramatically. Before the drive was over, more than 275,000 Americans were eager to help the cause and gave as generously as they could. Eventually the $7 million needed to build the memorial came—every dollar from the people. It "did not cost the government a dime,"[2] one journalist wrote, which was the way the VVMF wanted it.

To maintain their independence from bureaucratic red tape and delays, they had decided not to accept any government money for the memorial.

✳ 35 ✳

The VVMF made a timetable for their plan. It was brief:

- 1980—Obtain land for the memorial.
- 1981—Select a design and finish fundraising.
- 1982—Complete construction; conduct dedication on Veterans Day.

Let the Competition Begin

Many people told the VVMF that their timetable was impossible. No memorial had ever been built in such a short time as three years. But VVMF leaders were determined to do it. First they lobbied Congress, whose approval was needed for building the memorial on a two-acre tract of land on the National Mall. The National Mall is a park run by the National Park Service in the heart of Washington, DC. The Mall includes the land on which the Washington Monument, the Lincoln Memorial, and the US Capitol stand. Approximately twenty-four million people visit this site annually.

The portion of the National Mall on which the VVMF wanted to build the memorial was difficult to wrest from congressional control. Known as Constitution Gardens, it had been developed from a former swamp by a well-known landscape architect, Henry Arnold, in 1976. The purpose was to commemorate the bicentennial—the two-hundredth anniversary of the signing of the Declaration of Independence. Close to the Capitol, Constitution Gardens was a park-like setting with beautiful vistas.

Congress delayed and objected. It suggested locations outside the city for the monument. Standing firm, the

VVMF refused any location other than Constitution Gardens. Eventually, Congress gave in and granted approval.

Next came the selection of a design for the memorial. The VVMF decided to hold an open competition to help publicize the campaign. Jan Scruggs and his codirectors appointed a highly qualified panel of architects and landscape designers to judge the entries, and hoped for a design with a "powerful idea."[3]

The guidelines the VVMF sent out to those who inquired about the competition included several objectives. The primary one was Scruggs's: to have the names of all the war dead on the memorial. The other objectives were more general. The memorial should be in harmony with its location. That was prompted by John Wheeler's hope for a "landscape solution,"[4] a horizontal structure in a garden setting. The VVMF determined early on that it would not exclude any ideas or forms if they were powerful enough. Robert Doubek hoped for a monument that would "recognize and honor those who served and died . . . to begin a healing process."[5]

The competition got under way in the fall of 1980. With a deadline of four months away settled, the VVMF members had only to wait for the great design they hoped would emerge. They looked forward to seeing a design that would put into stone and marble their resolve to give the Vietnam War veterans the respect and honor that was long overdue.

A Challenge

At Yale University, the announcement of the competition came at an appropriate time. Professor Burr's class had just completed a seminar on funerary architecture, during which they had studied memorials and monuments for the dead. Outstanding war memorials in France built for the slain soldiers of World War I were especially noted. Most of those were erected where the great battles had raged—the Somme, Ypres, the Meuse-Argonne. They were awe-inspiring structures, rising over the thousands of graves of the soldiers killed there.

The subject of war memorials interested at least one student in Professor Burr's class. Maya Lin thought that creating a design for a modern war memorial was a "great idea."[6] However, she knew very little about the Vietnam War and the United States' involvement in it.

Lin was a small child when the fiercest battles raged in Vietnam. There were demonstrations against the war at Ohio University, as well as on many other American college campuses. Lin's parents kept their children inside during the riots and demonstrations in Athens. It wasn't until much later that she understood the significance of those events. The struggle in Southeast Asia that had created such tension, anger, and bitterness in the United States had been over for several years. Since the war ended, she had not read any books about it or seen any of the films that depicted the violence and bloodshed. She said once, "I hate war. All wars."[7]

While young American soldiers were dying in Vietnam, many back home took to the streets in protest. This photo shows an anti-Vietnam War peace march in San Francisco, California, in 1970.

Even during the competition, Maya Lin did not read about the Vietnam War. She did not want to be influenced by politics. But she did read a great deal about memorials and their meaning. In thinking about a memorial dedicated to the Vietnam War veterans, she said, "I felt a memorial should be honest about the reality of war, and be for the people who gave their lives."[8]

Remembrance, healing, reconciliation—all those should be represented in the memorial. But how? Lin read and reread the guidelines the VVMF had issued. Besides the definite requirement of having the names

An Unwinnable War

The country of Vietnam had been partitioned when the French, who had ruled it since 1885, were defeated by communist forces. North Vietnam was ruled by a communist government. Supported by communist China and the Soviet Union, North Vietnam's mission was to take over South Vietnam.

The South Vietnamese government was anti-Communist and pro-American. The United States' commitment to South Vietnam was explained by General William C. Westmoreland, who would become the commander of the American forces in Vietnam. It was "the desire of a strong nation to help an aspiring nation achieve independence."[9]

The United States' involvement in Vietnam began in 1959 in an extremely limited capacity, with only military advisers sent to help South Vietnam. By 1963, 16,000 American combat troops had been sent there. The numbers escalated every year. By the war's end, ten years later, 850,000 soldiers had served in the desperate cause.

The United States had failed in their mission: The guerrilla warfare waged by the North Vietnamese and their sympathizers from the South was never stopped. In 1973,

of those killed in the war inscribed on the monument, there was another condition that had great meaning for Lin. The memorial should be in harmony with its site—between the monuments that were Washington landmarks. The Lincoln Memorial itself symbolized reconciliation between North and South after the Civil War.

by an agreement known as the Paris Accords, the United States' involvement in the war in Vietnam was ended, and its troops began to withdraw.

The agreement was that the people of South Vietnam would decide on their own future government. But two years after the cease-fire, the North Vietnamese overran South Vietnam, and all remaining United States' personnel were evacuated, along with many South Vietnamese refugees. In 1976, the two sections of Vietnam were unified, and the country became known as the Socialist Republic of Vietnam.

The Vietnam War's toll was staggering: 58,000 American soldiers were killed or missing in action and 300,000 were wounded. More than two million men and women served time in Vietnam in noncombat roles. In Vietnam, millions of civilians were killed, wounded, uprooted from their homes, or exposed to deadly chemicals. Their children were orphaned. Agent Orange, a powerful defoliant meant to destroy plant life, was sprayed over many sections of the land by the United States' military. Its effects are still felt, not only by the Vietnamese but also by the American soldiers who were exposed to it.

What form should her design take? Lin still had no idea. But she knew she had to see the site.

Inspiration Strikes

After the Thanksgiving recess, Lin and several of her fellow students met at Constitution Gardens in Washington, DC. She saw at once that the VVMF was right. This beautiful landscape called for a memorial in harmony with it. She walked all over the site and took many photographs: the sloping ground, the background trees, the bright monuments in the distance. It was a quiet, peaceful place.

After a half hour, as she explained later, "The design sort of popped into my head. I wanted some sort of journey into the earth."[10] A rift in the earth was what she visualized, "with the memorial going into the ground, then emerging from it, symbolizing death and calling for remembrance."[11] She said that she "thought about what death is and what a loss is—a sharp pain that lessens with time but can never quite heal over. A scar. The idea occurred to me there on the site."[12]

Lin returned to Yale, and, as she remembers,

> I sketched the idea and worked it up in clay. It seemed almost too simple. Then I recalled . . . all the names of those killed and missing in action must be part of the memorial . . . the names would become the memorial. There was no need to embellish.[13]

The final result of her work was a pastel sketch of two black walls going into, then rising from, the earth against a background of trees and grass. Lin showed it to her classmates and asked for reactions from them and Professor Burr. The students wondered why the walls of the memorial were not white. Lin said that the black marble would give more reflection to the names.

Professor Burr suggested that the two walls on the design should come together to form an angle. Lin

Visiting the proposed site for the memorial helped Lin create her final design. Drawing inspiration from nature would prove important to her subsequent projects as well.

agreed with this and also with his suggestion that the names on the wall should be arranged chronologically by the date of death, not alphabetically. She saw how, by that logic, the names could come together to indicate the war's beginning and end. "The time sequence, which has the dates of the first and last deaths meeting at the intersection of these walls, is the essence of the design,"[14] she told the VVMF later.

Lin revised her design and mailed it to Washington. She was the only student in her class to submit an entry to the competition. Even as she sent it off, however, she herself had some doubts about it. Although she liked it, she felt that her design couldn't win. "It was too different, too strange,"[15] she said. Professor Burr thought it was "too strong,"[16] and graded it B but urged her to send it in anyway.

Washington Comes Calling

A month later, Lin was sitting in class when her roommate appeared at the door and passed a note to her. Washington had called, asking for Maya Lin. They would call again in fifteen minutes. Lin hurried to her room in time to get the second call. It was from Colonel Don Schaet, a staff member of the VVMF. "Don't get excited," he told Lin. "And please don't tell anyone about this call. We're coming up to talk to you."[17]

Such a message naturally made Lin wonder. Did it mean the possibility of an award—a minor one, maybe honorable mention? She waited. Later that day, three VVMF staff members arrived at Yale and met her in the dormitory. Don Schaet, who was a retired Marine Corps colonel, started by explaining how important the proposed memorial was. Lin listened. One of the other visitors said, "Come on. Tell her." Shaet nodded. "All right," he said. "You've won. First prize."[18]

If they expected to see Maya Lin jump up and down and scream with joy, they were disappointed. She said nothing, showed no emotion. Her very first feeling, she said later, was disbelief.[19] This could not be happening to her.

After the initial shock of the news wore off, she listened attentively to Colonel Schaet. She heard him ask if she could get down to Washington soon for a press conference. Lin could, the very next day. Although it was final exam time, she would postpone a scheduled exam.

After the visitors left, Lin tried to convince herself that she had really won first prize. That evening, she called her parents to tell them the news. Then she tried to sleep. The following day, she flew to Washington alone.

At the VVMF headquarters, she met the sponsors of the competition. They saw a woman—a college student—who looked even younger than her twenty-one years. In fact, Maya Lin did not look not much different from the Ohio teenager who had entered Yale as a freshman—small, slight, five feet three inches tall, and ninety pounds. She wore no makeup, and her hair was still long and hanging straight down her back.

The VVMF people liked her immediately, and applauded as she walked in. Lin smiled then. She finally began to believe what was happening. She began to believe that she had really won.

Chapter 5

CONTROVERSY ENSUES

Maya Lin did not have much time to adapt to her new situation. Things would move quickly, whether she wanted them to or not. She had a lot of work to do. But first, she would have to explain her well-thought-out design to a group of reporters at a press conference.

A model of the winning design was displayed at the first press conference held by the VVMF after the first-place selection was made. Lin explained her vision to the journalists present: The memorial would consist of two long walls, each more than two hundred feet long, coming together to form an angle like a triangle. Beginning underground and rising to a height of ten feet, the walls would meet at the apex of the triangle. They would be inscribed with the names of the nearly fifty-eight thousand Americans confirmed dead in the Vietnam War.

As Lin and Professor Burr had decided, the names would be in chronological, not alphabetical, order, grouped according to the dates of death. At the press conference, she explained that a traditional alphabetical arrangement would put the same names together. For example, there were over six hundred Smiths among the casualties, and sixteen people named James Jones. That arrangement would make the memorial look "like a telephone book engraved in granite."[1] Putting the names in chronological order would draw together the comrades killed at the same time, often in the same battle. Lin had

Lin holds a scale model of her design for the Vietnam Veterans' Memorial in 1981. The university student would have to present the design to journalists at a press conference.

already convinced VVMF that this idea was the most logical.

Lin also explained to the journalists why the memorial should be black marble instead of white, like most of the other memorials in Washington. Besides reflecting the names better, black marble could be polished to give a mirror-like image of the Mall and the people looking at the names. The effect would be as if people and the names came together. In a later interview, Lin said that "the color black is a lot more peaceful and gentle than white. White marble may be very beautiful, but you can't read anything on it."[2]

Privacy in a Public World

The journalists wrote up their articles, and details of the monument plans were published in newspapers around the country. Lin received a great deal of publicity. Interviewed several times, she was forthcoming and cooperative, and gave out quite a few details about her life and family.

She was described by Jonathan Coleman in *Time* as "shy, yet affable, serious but quick to smile, and full of energy."[3] As time went on, however, Lin would not welcome the continued publicity, especially from the merely curious. "Her private life is something she guards fiercely,"[4] Coleman commented later.

After the VVMF announced the award, Lin's father in Athens, Ohio, was asked what he thought of his daughter's winning design. He described it as "simple, yet

Lin stands with Scruggs in front of model memorial walls during a news conference in 1981.

very direct,"[5] somewhat Chinese, he believed, in that her family culture might be said to reflect in her work.

Although in later years, Lin conceded that her artistic outlook was "distinctly Asian,"[6] at this point, she identified more strongly with her American heritage. She said, "I don't speak or write Chinese,"[7] and her mother commented that, "Maya is so modern in so many ways. She considers herself much more American than Chinese."[8] Mrs. Lin's influence was noted when her daughter described the design that won the judges' admiration as "visual poetry"[9] and later said that the Wall (as the memorial became known) "could be read like an epic Greek poem."[10]

A Controversial Memorial for an Unpopular War

After the description of Lin's design was made public, however, differences of opinion about it arose. Not everybody admired the choice of the judges and the art world "elite." The criticism grew and soon a controversy began between those who favored modern art, as Lin's design was labeled, and those who disliked it. Modern art is often abstract and difficult to understand. It portrays ideas and impressions rather than a realistic representation of what is familiar. Traditional art depicts scenes and portraits as they might be in life, or as they are "represented."

Opponents of Maya Lin's design wanted a traditional monument in keeping with the familiar ones positioned around Washington—statues of famous figures, heroes on horseback, and familiar shapes in white marble. A stark, unadorned set of black walls with names instead of symbols was abstract to many people.

The memorial to be was called "unheroic" because it would be partly below ground level; a "black gash of shame"; a "degrading ditch"; a "wailing wall for Vietnam War protesters"; and more. The architecture critic of a leading newspaper said, "The so-called memorial is bizarre, neither a building nor sculpture."[11]

Maya Lin, upset by the criticism, said scathingly, "Modern art makes a lot of people nervous."[12] She hoped people would not close their minds to the memorial before they saw it completed. In fact, one of the judges of the competition had foreseen the negative reaction.

Defending Lin's Design

Many years after the Vietnam Veterans Memorial was built, Maya Lin wrote, "Perhaps it was an empathetic response to the idea about war that led me to cut open the earth—an initial violence that heals in time but leaves a memory, like a scar. But this imagery, which some detractors would later describe as "a black gash of shame and sorrow" in which the color black was called the "universal color of shame and dishonor," would prove incredibly difficult to defend . . . .It took a prominent four-star general, Brigadier General George Price, who happened to be black, testifying before one of the countless subcommittee hearings and defending the color black, before the design could move forward."[13]

He said "many people would not understand the design until they experienced it."[14]

Maya Lin herself never lost faith in the integrity of her work. She was sure her design would result in the right kind of memorial for those who had sacrificed their lives as well as for those who mourned them. Several years later, Lin said, "I knew that if that project was built, it would help. I cannot answer why I knew that. I'd never known anyone who died. All I knew was that if we could face death, face it honestly, only then can we get over it." [15]

Accepting the Judges' Choice

When they first looked at the design, Jan Scruggs and his fellow directors of the VVMF did not quite know what to say. They had listened to the judges' description of the winning entry. Maya Lin, the experts said, had created "an eloquent place where the simple setting of earth, sky and remembered names" come together.[16] The design would result in a "monument for our times."[17] It would be harmonious with its site, "entering the earth rather than piercing the sky."[18] The VVMF listened and agreed, but still—they wondered.

Jan Scruggs kept staring at this strange thing that his organization had brought into existence. At first it seemed to him a weird design.[19] But as he stood silently, brooding, he saw that those massive walls, longer than a football field when built, would contain the fifty-eight thousand names, all of them. He was satisfied. "It's a great memorial," he said.[20]

It was planned that most of the wall would be below grade, resulting in the appearance of the wall emerging from the earth. From above it was supposed to look like a scar in the ground.

John Wheeler and Robert Doubek both had second thoughts the longer they looked at the design. "I was surprised," Doubek recalled. "We were silent for a moment. But when we understood . . . the genius of the simple concept, it took effect on us. We embraced and congratulated each other. We were thrilled."[21]

True to Her Vision

When opponents of the design finally realized that they could not replace it with another, they demanded changes or additions to it. At the very least, they wanted a statue and a flag. Lin protested. She was against any additions to the memorial. The names were enough.

"If you want to change something, reconvene the jury," she said defiantly. [22] She resisted the idea of a flag being placed on the memorial because it was her belief that, as the guidelines of the competition read, the memorial should avoid making a political statement. The names were enough. "I'll be stubborn about that,"[23] she said, and she was. Besides, as she said, a flag would make the site "look like a golf green."[24]

The opposition to the design was keeping the VVMF from completing the final step of their timetable. Even worse, it might prevent the memorial from being built at all. The secretary of the interior, whose department included the National Park Service and whose permission was necessary before construction could be started, sided with those protesting the design.

Realizing that the entire memorial was at risk, the VVMF directors decided to compromise. They were willing to add a statue and a flag, but not on the memorial itself. The secretary of the interior and other influential opponents of Maya Lin's design accepted the compromise.

The VVMF hired the sculptor Frederick Hart to create a statue. Hart had won third place in the design competition. He began his work on a realistic statue of three servicemen in the Vietnam War, which was to be ready for dedication in 1984.

However, the VVMF had not consulted Maya Lin about their action. When she heard of it, she was angry, and made her feelings known. She said she had been treated like a child,[25] overlooked on a matter that was vital to "her" memorial. She called the placing of a statue at the memorial like "drawing mustaches on other people's portraits."[26]

Jan Scruggs, whose driving motive had always been to get the fifty-eight thouand names on the memorial, said that the compromise was "the only way to get Maya Lin's piece built."[27] The Fine Arts Commission and many well-known architects agreed that Lin's memorial design itself should not be compromised. Scruggs promised that it would be done in such a way so as to not detract from her design. The VVMF agreed to place the proposed statue and flag at a considerable distance from the memorial.

Lin had also initially disagreed with the VVMF about placing an inscription that honored *all* the Vietnam veterans on the Wall. Lin firmly believed that nothing should be on the memorial but the names of those killed in the war. But the VVMF pointed out that the 2.7 million men and women who had served in Vietnam over the course of the war deserved some recognition. As it was impossible to have all those names on the memorial, an inscription would satisfy the VVMF's wish to honor them. Lin agreed, and an inscription in two parts—a prologue and an epilogue—was placed at the Wall's beginning and end, urging visitors to remember the courage and dedication of all those who served in the war.

The VVMF had originally wanted the inscription to be in large gilt letters. Kent Cooper, an architect from the firm Lin worked with on the project, rejected that idea. "No word, no letter should be more noticeable than any name," he said.[28] And so the final inscription did not overshadow the names.

Maya Lin remained true to her belief that nothing—including her own name—should go on the face of the memorial except the names. Instead, Lin's name is behind the memorial, out of public view, along with the names of the other people who were instrumental in building the Wall.

Chapter 6

BUILDING THE MEMORIAL

Maya Lin moved to Washington, DC, the day of her graduation from Yale. She was needed immediately to help navigate the process of acquiring government approval for her design. She also would need to supervise the building of the memorial.

Despite the doubts expressed by those opposed to her design, she was determined to see her vision through: "I think my age made it seem apparent to some that I was too young to understand what I had done or see it through to completion."[1] She lived with two designer friends from Yale in an old ramshackle row house on Capitol Hill. In her spare time, she helped her friends remodel the house.

Describing that time twenty years later, Lin wrote,

> To bring the design into reality would require that I associate with an architect of record, a qualified firm that would work with me to realize the design. I had a very difficult time convincing the fund in charge of the memorial—the Vietnam Veterans Memorial Fund—of the importance of selecting a qualified firm that had experience both in architecture and landscape-integrated solutions, and that would be sympathetic to the design.[2]

Once again, Lin prevailed.

Working With Architects

Beginning in the summer of 1981, Lin worked as a consultant with Cooper-Lecky. She had persuaded the VVMF to partner with this architectural firm to develop the Vietnam memorial design. Many practical matters had to be considered before the design could even become a blueprint. The walls had to be made longer than in Lin's original design; the many names to be included needed even more room than she had calculated.

Then, with the contractor who had been hired and the landscape architect Henry Arnold, Lin walked all over Constitution Gardens to determine exactly where to place the memorial. It was important to have it in correct alignment with the imposing monuments on each side. Drainage problems and the water level of the site had to be considered also.

Lin had said after she won the competition that she didn't know how to draft. She learned that summer, along with some other nitty-gritty details of construction. Although she was on hand for "consultation" regarding the work on the memorial, Lin also did whatever an apprentice architect was assigned to do. One of her jobs was designing water fountains for the upcoming New Orleans Exposition.

Although Lin accepted that she was learning, she never forgot that it was *her* work the architects were dealing with in their design development. She vetoed any attempt to change the original design. She sometimes felt that she was being treated as the greenest, most inexperienced of beginners. She said the attitude of the architects was, "All right, you've done the design. It's real simple. We'll take it from there."[3] That, she decided was not going to happen. The design was hers, every aspect of it, so she did not hesitate to express her opinions. And the architects that she had fought so hard to have on the project wisely listened when they realized that this extraordinary young woman had a clarity of vision for her design. "I decided on everything, from the lettering to the sandblasting, to the alphabet style of the inscription," she said.[4]

Lin's experiences that year convinced her that architecture "is a very male-dominated profession," but she added, "I intend to succeed in it"[5] and to prove that "women can get things built."[6] She planned to continue studying architecture in graduate school and to eventually open her own office as a professional architect.

Lin relocated to Washington DC for the building of the memorial. She was photographed visiting the construction site in July 1982.

Constructing Commences

Once the controversy over the statue and the flag was settled—it was called Lin's "baptism by fire"[7]—the building of the memorial could begin. Bulldozers opened up the ground in March 1982, and the massive job got underway. The black granite for the walls came from India. Then it was shipped to Vermont, and stonecutters cut it into panels. These were polished to a high luster. From Vermont the panels went to Tennessee, where skilled workmen sandblasted the names of those killed or missing in action on them.

Arranging the names beforehand had been a long, complicated process. The correct names of the

The Politics of Art

The Vietnam War was highly controversial. Many Americans protested the United States' involvement in the war, and specifically the draft, or the involuntary selection of young men by the government, to serve in the armed forces.

Although Lin had made a personal decision to keep politics out of her memorial, it was perhaps inevitable that the deeply rooted controversy would embed itself in the project. " One aspect that made the project unusual was its politicized building process. For instance, the granite could not come from Canada or Sweden. Though those countries had beautiful black granites, draft evaders went to both countries [to avoid having to serve in the war], so the veterans felt that we could not consider their granites as options."[8]

servicemen had been researched along with their tours of duty. Then they were placed on the panels in the proper chronological order. That arrangement was an important part of Maya Lin's design. She had stated in the design's explanation that the names would begin and end in the center of the memorial, where the walls would meet. The name of the first person killed in the war would be inscribed at the top of one wall and the names of others would follow down to the end of that wall. On the other wall, the names would continue at the bottom and go upward until the last casualty's name was at the top, meeting the name of the first one. Thus, Maya said, "the war's beginning and end meet; the war is complete, coming full circle."[9]

The names of those soldiers missing in action were included with the names of those who had been killed. A small symbol next to each name indicates whether a person named is officially confirmed killed or is missing in action. The names of those who were killed in action are followed by a diamond. Those missing are denoted with a cross. It was agreed that the symbol of any missing-in-action servicemen who were confirmed dead at some future time would be changed to reflect their new status.

Room was left on the panels of the walls to add more names when necessary—names of those who died later as a result of war-caused wounds. Periodically, names are still added to the others on the Wall. The families of those servicemen make sure of that. Having a name inscribed on the Wall is an honor and a recognition, and,

Despite critics' first impressions, it soon became clear that Lin's choice of material and design would create dramatic impact.

as Lin herself said, "The name is one of the most magical ways to bring back a person."[10]

The dedication of the Wall took place as scheduled in the VVMF's timetable—on Veterans Day, 1982. The day was only eight months after the actual construction was started. It was a remarkable feat. No other Washington Monument had been built in such a short time.

The Power of the Wall

More than thirty years after the memorial was built, the sheer enormity of the number of names on the Wall is still so striking that at first it silences the people who see it. As people draw near to see the names, they touch and often they cry. The meaning of all those names is not lost.

The near-universal effect of seeing the names on the Wall is as Lin predicted it would be. When Lin went there as a visitor for the first time, she said, "I searched out the name of a friend's father. I touched it and I cried. I was another visitor, and I was reacting to it as I had designed it."[11]

Maya Lin's intention in designing the memorial was realized, just as Jan Scruggs's was. For Scruggs, it was to see all fifty-eight thousand names on a memorial that would stand forever. For Lin, the Wall was an honest reflection about the reality of war by listing the names of those who gave their lives for it: "Each name [is] a special human being who never came home."[12] Although the memorial intentionally made no political statement

A Vietnam veteran weeps after locating his friend's name. The monument elicits powerful reactions from those who visit it.

about the Vietnam War, the names alone "come across as a powerful antiwar statement."[13]

Writer Arthur C. Danto described the Wall as "a book of the dead, listed in chronological order from the first one killed in 1959 to the last one in 1975."[14] Maya Lin's "Book of the Dead" can be read by everyone who visits the Wall.

In spite of her frustration about the controversy over the design and the attempts to make changes to it, Lin had seen her vision through. Her concept of a memorial befitting war veterans had been built just as she had imagined. Many people had been associated with the project of building the memorial, and many had opposed it—but it was Maya Lin's name that would be remembered.

The memorial was hers, unique and elegant, powerful and simple, different from memorials of the past. This one, stark and unadorned, with names instead of symbols, is the monument of today. It has influenced the style of many other memorials in cities and states across the country. More than four million people visit the Vietnam Veterans Memorial every year.

Chapter 7

Moving On From The Wall

Despite her involvement in the construction of the Wall, Lin was eager to continue her graduate studies. She enrolled in Harvard University's Graduate School of Design while construction of the Wall was still in progress. Every weekend she commuted from Cambridge, Massachusetts, to Washington, DC, where she checked into a hotel. She worked on her university assignments at night and on memorial problems during the day.

However, the pressure of trying to manage two full-time endeavors became unbearable. After staying up all night to finish a school paper, she decided, "I can't do this any more."[1] She quit her graduate work at Harvard, and soon after the dedication of the memorial, she left Washington, DC, a city she had come to dislike.

In a gesture of frustration and perhaps to look older, she chopped off her long hair. Lin was self-conscious about her youthful appearance, which prevented some people from taking her seriously. She told Jonathan Coleman of *Time* that she was looking forward to becoming thirty.[2]

A New Start

Lin moved to one of her favorite cities, Boston, and signed on with an architectural firm there. For the next year, she worked as an apprentice. She helped design houses and, on her own, designed a stage set in Philadelphia.

The Vietnam Veterans Memorial was dedicated on November 13, 1982. At the dedication, Lin was photographed in front of crowds of people honoring friends and relatives who served in the war.

The various projects in which she was involved gave her practical experience and prepared her for further study.

By the fall of 1983, Lin was ready to return to academic life. She decided to go back to Yale, her alma mater. "I needed a place to start over," she told a reporter who interviewed her for *Newsweek*. "Yale was like going home."[3]

At Yale, Lin studied architecture under two renowned professors, Frank Gehry and Vincent Tully. Professor Tully was an architectural historian who greatly admired Lin's Vietnam Veterans Memorial. He called it a "moving," and "remarkable" monument.[4]

The Memorial Is Expanded

Two years after the memorial's dedication, on Veterans Day 1984, the Vietnam memorial was again prominent in the news. Frederick Hart's statue was unveiled and formally dedicated. It was, as required, located well away from the Wall.

The memorial now included the Wall, Hart's statue, and a large American flag atop a fifty-foot pole near the entrance plaza to the site. The memorial was turned over to the National Park Service and thus became the responsibility of the US government to maintain.

The statue is a larger-than-life bronze depiction of three young servicemen who wear the uniform and equipment of war. They stand looking tired and weary, as if gazing across a field, or as some visitors think, looking at the Wall commemorating the dead. A writer who described the statue thus said that the two parts of

Lin fought the addition of *The Three Servicemen* statue, because she believed it would detract from the impact of the memorial.

the memorial "were not separate—they seemed made for reconciliation."[5]

Afterward, Lin said, "In a funny sense, the compromise brings the memorial closer to the truth. What is also memorialized is that people still cannot resolve that war, nor can they separate the issues, the politics, from it."[6]

Lin did not attend the 1984 dedication of the statue. Many people were not aware of the controversy over the statue and Lin's objection to it. Benjamin Forgey, a *Washington Post* reporter, wrote that Lin's name "unpardonably went unmentioned in the ceremony, but her presence was there for all to see: the great black wall, rising from and returning to grass-covered earth, exactly on axis with the Washington Monument and the Lincoln Memorial."[7]

Expanding Her Vision

Between academic semesters Lin spent time with her family. She traveled to Paris to see her brother, who was studying there. In 1985, she went to China with her parents. She also worked as an apprentice to a Japanese architect in Tokyo.

Back home, she wrote about some of her architectural experiences in Asia. *The New Republic* published her article about outstanding new buildings in Hong Kong, skyscrapers that she said break from the more traditional style by being innovative, "futuristic . . . representing the 21st Century."[8] Some existing New York City skyscrapers she criticized as "inhuman, lifeless, monotonous," housing nothing more than "compartments."[9] Her opinions were clearly expressed and informative, revealing her own leaning toward the daringly new and modern style.

In 1986, Maya Lin was awarded a master's degree in architecture from Yale University. Just a year later, when she was only twenty-seven, Yale bestowed on her the honorary degree of doctor of fine arts. She was already one of the university's foremost alumna.

Keeping a Low Profile

Around this time, Lin moved to New York City, where she established her permanent base in an old loft building in the Bowery, on the city's lower East Side. The building housed several other artists, most of them friends Lin had known at Yale. She shared a studio apartment with a companion.

Here, six flights up, Lin felt safe from curiosity seekers who would not expect a famous artist to be living in a nondescript building on the Bowery. Only a cat or two might wander in from the street to be adopted by the loft's tenants.

Lin valued her privacy. Being a celebrity was not something she sought. In fact, as she told Elizabeth Kastor of *The Washington Post,* she never wanted to be "troubled by fame."[10] Here in her chosen lifestyle, surrounded by other artists and friends, Lin could work quietly on her sculptures in a studio awash with blueprints, plans, and scale models, the walls covered with photos and sketches. She could dress casually, comfortably in her usual self-described "thrift shop originals"[11] of jeans, sneakers, and a rumpled jacket.

Portrait of the Artist

Lin always considered herself an artist even after she chose to study architecture. At graduate school, professors suggested that she should choose between the two. As she says, however, "I can't deny the other side of me."[12]

She told Jill Kirschenbaum of *Ms.* that architecture is like writing a book, sculpture like composing a poem.[13] Sculpture is poetry in that it is one idea "stripped bare," whereas architecture is composed of many related ideas.

The sculptures that engrossed Lin when she was not designing architecture were, as Peter Tauber said, "slow to be made and quick to sell."[14] Composed of some of Lin's favorite materials—lead, broken glass, and mottled beeswax—one piece might take a year to complete. Her sculptures were on display at such well-regarded venues as the Sidney Janis Gallery and other galleries in New York City.

Lin received many requests for public appearances and lectures, most of which she turned down. It was not in her interest to become a celebrity or art world darling. One that she accepted in 1990 was at the Metropolitan Museum of Art in New York City. She told the overflow audience who came to hear her that "architects call me a sculptor and sculptors call me an architect." And she added humorously, "I don't think either one wants to claim me."[15]

What About the Women?

In the meantime in Washington, DC, another controversy about a statue was emerging. A group of women who had served with the American forces during the years of the Vietnam War decided that they also deserved a statue on the site of the Vietnam Veterans Memorial.

To achieve this goal, they organized the Vietnam Women's Memorial Project (VWMP). Their aim was to have a statue honoring the women—all 250,000—who had been participants in some phase of the war effort. Ninety percent of those women were nurses, about 10,000 served in the armed forces, and the rest were volunteers in the USO and Red Cross. The eight women who were killed in Vietnam—all nurses—have their names on the Wall.

It took several years for the VWMP to achieve their goal of having a memorial statue for the Vietnam War's women veterans. Although the secretary of the interior

Women Vietnam War Veterans

The nurses of the United States Army Nurses Corps who served in Vietnam had seen firsthand all the horrors of the war. Their experiences in Vietnam affected them deeply; many were emotionally scarred. Like the men who were in combat, they too suffered for years afterward from post-traumatic stress disorder (PTSD), and many of them were helped to recover at the center set up in Menlo Park, New Jersey, by the Veterans Administration.

approved the women's application to have their statue at Constitution Gardens, strong opposition arose about that location.

Chief among the opponents was J. Carter Brown, the head of the Capitol's Fine Arts Commission. He had sided with Maya Lin when she objected to having *The Three Servicemen* statue on the same site as the Wall. Commissioner Brown said the Vietnam memorial was "symbolically complete,"[16] and the placing of another statue near the Wall would encourage other organizations to follow suit. "It will never end,"[17] he predicted.

The influential Washington, DC, newspaper, *The Washington Post,* kept abreast of the controversy. Journalist Benjamin Forgey wrote, "If we begin to single out veterans by gender, why not select them by ethnic group . . . by specialties such as engineers, pilots, sergeants?"[18]

An editorial in the *Post* agreed, declaring that although the plan to have a women's memorial was praiseworthy, the statue should be in another place. "Separate statues for special groups would detract from the whole," the *Post* argued, and continued, "Congress should leave this work of art alone."[19]

Many members of Congress endorsed the VWMF's desire to locate their statue on the site that the women wanted. But because of the opposition, Congress decided to hold hearings on the subject. Maya Lin returned to Washington, DC, in February 1988 to defend the position taken by the Fine Arts Commission.

In the hearing, she maintained that the site of the Wall, being already complete, should not have any further additions imposed on it. She said that if this latest attempt to add another statue to the memorial was allowed, "It would be tampering with a national monument already approved."[20]

Congress delayed, and the arguments pro and con continued. The VWMP kept pressing for the site they wanted. They finally won their campaign when Congress voted to allow them to build a memorial statue on federal land. President Ronald Reagan signed the bill.

A year later, in November 1989, President George H.W. Bush signed legislation authorizing the placing of the statue within what is designated as "Area 1" of the Mall. That was the site of the Vietnam Veterans Memorial.

In 1990, the Fine Arts Commission and the Memorial Planning Commission granted approval for the designated site, reluctantly. But a compromise of sorts was arranged. Although the statue was to be on the Vietnam Veterans Memorial grounds, it was to be as far from the Wall as possible—three hundred feet southeast of *The Three Servicemen* statue.

The women veterans' memorial was completed by the sculptor Glenna Goodacre of New Mexico, and was dedicated on Veterans Day, 1993. It is called a "multifigure sculpture in the round, portraying three Vietnam-era women, one of whom is caring for a wounded male

The Vietnam Women's Memorial commemorates the women—mostly nurses—who were instrumental in the conflict. The statue depicts three women in uniform attending to a wounded soldier.

soldier."[21] As described, "the statue will overlook the names etched on the wall."[22]

In her *New York Times Magazine* article about the nurses of Vietnam, Laura Palmer wrote that, on Veterans Day, 1993, "a nation that never really noticed and hardly seemed to care . . . finally honored them with a memorial of their own."[23]

Except from the air, Maya Lin did not see the Vietnam Veterans Memorial for several years after she left Washington, DC. As time went on however, in spite of the addition of the statues, she could feel satisfaction over her own accomplishment in creating the great centerpiece on the Mall.

Chapter 8

A Second Memorial

fter Lin completed the Vietnam Veterans Memorial, she said that she would never design another war memorial.[1] The political controversy over her design had discouraged her. "I think it is actually a miracle that the piece ever got built,"[2] she wrote years later.

Lin retreated into her private life, did her own kind of work—sculptures—and accepted some private commissions, which she discovered she liked. "I'm interested in the psychology of the client,"[3] she said.

The Right Architect

In the spring of 1988, Lin was at work in her loft studio when she received a call from a representative of the Southern Poverty Law Center of Montgomery, Alabama, known as the SPLC. The organization had been founded in 1971 to protect and advance the legal rights of poor people and minorities.

The board of directors, headed by Morris Dees, the founder, had decided that they wanted a civil rights memorial on the plaza adjacent to their headquarters in Montgomery. One of the SPLC trustees said they should commission a top-notch architect for the job. The name of Maya Lin came immediately to mind. Her address in New York was not known then to the SPLC, and as Morris Dees recalled, "we phoned every Lin in the New York phone book"[4] before Maya Lin was reached.

Lin did not immediately agree to design the memorial, but she did say she would read the material the SPLC

Lin designed the memorial to honor those who died during the Civil Rights Movement. A quote from Martin Luther King Jr. inspired the water feature on which the names of those who died are carved.

wished to send her and would consider the matter. She took some time to do this, and then she decided to accept the commission.

The historical significance of the civil rights movement impressed her. She was surprised that there was no such memorial already in existence. She was also concerned that she knew so little about the movement, never having studied it in school. She was a very young child during the 1960s when the marches and the landmark decisions had occurred, and only eight when Martin Luther King Jr. was assassinated.

Lin said that although there were specific monuments to certain people connected with the civil rights movement, "No memorial existed that encompassed the movement itself and caught what the whole era was about. It had been very much a people's movement—many people gave their lives for it, and that had been largely forgotten."[5]

After agreeing to design the memorial, Lin went to see the site. On the plane to Montgomery, she reread some of the words of Dr. King. She came across—not for the first time—what he said in several of his speeches. "We will not be satisfied until justice rolls down like waters, and righteousness like a mighty stream."[6] The words are taken from the book of Amos in the Old Testament.

"Suddenly," Lin said, "something clicked," and the form took shape. "The minute I hit that quote I knew that the whole piece had to be about water."[7] The longer she considered it, the more certain she was. "I wanted to work with water, and I wanted to use the words [of Dr. King] because that's the clearest way to remember history."[8]

Lin kept thinking about the form of the memorial as she continued her journey. It occurred to her that in the warm climate of Alabama, the cooling effect of flowing water would be appropriate. When she met the members of the SPLC at lunch in Montgomery, she quickly sketched what she had in mind on a paper napkin. After lunch, at the site where the memorial would stand, Lin saw the possibilities—and the need for rearranging some existing features there. It was agreed that she would start on the design as soon as she returned to New York.

The Center of the Civil Rights Movement

Montgomery was a meaningful city for establishing a civil rights memorial. Just a few blocks away from the site was the Dexter Avenue Baptist Church, were Dr. Martin Luther King Jr. had preached. Montgomery was also the place where in 1965 the famous march from Selma ended. Led by Dr. King, that march was a demonstration on behalf of civil and voting rights for black people.

Before that, in 1955, Montgomery was in the headlines as the place where Rosa Parks, riding on a city bus, refused to give up her seat to a white person and was arrested. The result was a boycott of the public buses in Montgomery by black people, also led by Dr. King. The boycott went on for over a year, during which no black persons in Montgomery rode the city buses. Finally, the

US Supreme Court ruled in favor of the protesters and outlawed bus segregation.

Morris Dees and his organization fought the Klu Klux Klan in court many times over the years. Lawsuits were won by the SPLC against the Klan for its hate crimes and attacks on civil rights leaders and buildings.

The SPLC sponsors various projects to fight racial violence. Among them are Klanwatch, which takes legal action against offenders, and Teaching Tolerance, which develops educational materials and distributes them across America. To show her commitment to the cause, Maya Lin became a member of the advisory board of the SPLC's Teaching Tolerance project.

Designing the Memorial

The Southern Poverty Law Center's plan in 1988 was to memorialize those individuals who had been killed in the course of marches and demonstrations for civil rights. On the memorial, their names and the names of landmark events in the civil rights struggle would be etched in stone.

The research of records was done by Sara Bullard, one of the directors of the SPLC and the editor of the Center's book about the civil rights movement, *Free at Last*. Fifty-three significant entries would be inscribed on the memorial.

When Lin saw that list, she said she realized that creating a time line was the way to highlight those names and events. They would be listed in chronological order from the first—"17 May 1954, the Supreme Court ruling outlawing school segregation" to the last, "4 April 1968, Martin Luther King Jr., assassinated." There would be room at both ends for additions if related names and events were discovered.

Back in her studio, Lin started work on the project. The memorial she had decided to design would be in two parts and was scheduled to be dedicated in the fall of 1989. There would be a huge granite disk, or table, twelve feet in diameter, inscribed with the fifty-three names and events. The table, with the names arranged chronologically in a circle around the perimeter, would look something like a sundial. Behind the large disk there would be a black

At the 1989 dedication of the Civil Rights Memorial, Lin was photographed standing on the balcony of the the Southern Poverty Law Center overlooking her monument.

granite wall, nine feet high, which would be inscribed with the words of Dr. King that had inspired Lin's design.

In the completed memorial, water flows down the wall in a gentle cascade over those words. The table below the wall was designed to be less than three feet from the ground, made low so that children could reach it. The table, narrower at the bottom, from a distance appears to be floating in air. Water rises from the center of the table and spreads over it, washing over the time line of names and events, which are still clearly seen through the thin veil of water. Visitors would be expected to touch the names as they walked around the table.

The Civil Rights Memorial was dedicated on time, although it had been complicated and difficult to construct. Ken Upchurch, who supervised the construction, said, when he first viewed the design, it was a "contractor's nightmare."[9] The day before the memorial was to be unveiled, the workers as well as the anxious SPLC people wondered if the water was going to work as well as it was supposed to. Last-minute adjustments took the workmen well into the night.

Then, when the memorial was finally, hopefully, ready, all those present held their breath as the water was turned on. A cheer went up when the water began its slow movement down the wall and across the table. Ken Upchurch said, "It worked perfectly."[10] A native of Montgomery, Upchurch said he learned more about the civil rights movement from constructing the memorial than he ever had before.

Near Disaster

In the fall of 1988, not long after Lin had completed the civil rights memorial design, fire broke out in the New York City building where she lived and worked. Fortunately, she had mailed the model of the memorial she'd made to the SPLC in Montgomery.

But before the fire was brought under control, much of the work of the artists who lived in the loft building was destroyed. Most of Maya Lin's sculptures were in the Sidney Janis Gallery, so her loss was minimal.

As Maya Lin explained to Elizabeth Kastor, who interviewed her shortly after the fire,[11] she, like many other artists, often destroyed a finished sculpture or other work if for some reason, she was not satisfied with it. She would start over. So would her friends. No one was injured in the fire, and the building was quickly repaired.

A Powerful Memorial

Besides being visited by families, friends, and relatives of those whose names are etched on it, the memorial attracts people from all over the country and the world. Tourists stop off in Montgomery to see it. As Lin had hoped, the memorial has become an educational experience. Students come, experience, and learn.

Lin, who aimed always for simplicity, said of the Civil Rights Memorial, "A child can understand it. You don't need to read an art history book to understand it."[12] One little girl said, "It makes you want to touch the names with your fingers, and talk about what happened."[13]

Like touching the names on the Vietnam Wall, this memorial, too, evokes tears from the many people who visit it. Lin was impressed, as she said, with the powerful effect that "words joined with water would generate."[14] She was "surprised and moved when people started to cry . . . tears were becoming part of the memorial, as William Zinsser wrote in *Smithsonian*."[15]

Lin received unqualified praise for her part in this memorial. Unlike the Vietnam Veterans Memorial, this one was happily free from controversy over its merits. One writer commented, "She has once again created an architectural masterpiece."[16] Lin herself said, "I've been

Visitors are encouraged to touch the memorial and reflect upon the lives lost during the struggle to achieve equal rights. Water washes over their names, representing the healing properties of water.

incredibly fortunate to have been given the opportunity to work on not just one but both memorials."[17]

Morris Dees said about the memorial she created for the Southern Poverty Law Center, "You can't put something better located than Montgomery, where everything happened, and you can't get anyone better than Maya Lin to do it."[18]

Chapter 9

LANDSCAPE PAINTER

As successful as the Vietnam Veterans and the Civil Rights Memorials were, Maya Lin did not want to be labeled as a memorial designer. There was a great deal she wanted to do, and a whole career lay ahead of her.

Years later, Lin would say, ". . . had I not done the Vietnam Memorial and come out with the body of work that has since come out, I would have been able to be called an artist five years sooner. But because I had done the Vietnam Memorial, it was like, 'Oh, you make monuments,' whatever that means."[1]

Peace Chapel

Lin had always had a strong interest in landscape architecture. Late in 1989, she accepted the first of what would ultimately be several important outdoor design commissions. Her first landscape design was for a Peace Chapel at Juniata College in Huntingdon, Pennsylvania.

Elizabeth Evans Baker and John Baker, the donors of the chapel, were friends of Lin's parents. Mr. Baker had been the president of Ohio University from 1945 to 1961, during the time that Julia and Henry Lin had joined the faculty there. The two families were good friends.

After Mr. Baker retired from Ohio University, he and his wife devoted themselves to the cause of world peace. They established the department of peace studies at Juniata, where Mr. Baker, a graduate of the college in 1917, served on the board of trustees.

Maya Lin said that she would never have envisioned doing this landscape project if Mrs. Baker had not asked her to design an open-air chapel for Juniata College. "It was the relationship of the two families"[2] and also, Lin said, the college's concern for world peace that brought her to Juniata.

The Peace Chapel was to be an open-air place where people could go for contemplation and for nondenominational church services. The location, about a mile from the college, was a protected bird sanctuary, owned and preserved by Juniata.

Maya Lin said that Mrs. Baker's ideas for an open-air chapel at this place "interested me from the start."[3] When she went to Huntingdon to inspect the site of the proposed chapel, she saw that she could not improve upon the location, a beautiful meadow set into the surrounding hills overlooking the college. It was a perfect place for the Peace Chapel.

The choice of Maya Lin as the architect was praised by Juniata's community—faculty and alumni alike. It was noted in the October 1989 alumni bulletin that the young artist's talent in relating a structure to its site was outstanding. The Vietnam Veterans Memorial was known as "a great work of landscape architecture," and one of the nation's "most respected works of public art."[4]

Lin designed the Peace Chapel in two parts. The first consisted of a large circle of roughhewn stones, huge blocks on which people would sit. The circle, forty feet in diameter, as Lin explained at the dedication ceremony, is a form that denotes symmetry and equality. Everyone sitting around it would be equal, with no arrangement that would rank or separate the group. "A very simple design," she said.[5]

The second part of the chapel reflects the first. It is a smaller circle, only five feet in diameter, set on a ridge, several feet above the first ring. Overlooking the larger circle, it is designed for private or individual reflection. Rough stones similar to the lower ones form the small circle. "One person can quietly sit there and contemplate, think . . . the two-part design frames the two ways in which we think, in which we gather," Lin explained.[6]

Juniata College's Peace Chapel carries out Maya Lin's basic ideas about the relationship between structures and land. Buildings that seem to grow from the earth, framed by the landscape, become part of it.

The roughhewn stones of the Peace Chapel, deliberately chosen to avoid a "manicured" look, will in time, Lin said, be covered with moss and surrounded by grass. There will be "quietly implied order,"[7] in harmony with nature. Maya Lin's feeling for simplicity is notable, never more so than in this open-air chapel.

As writer Peter Tauber commented, "Sometimes the most important lesson at a site is understanding what

Lin designed the Baker Peace Chapel, an installation at Juniata College in Huntingdon, Pennsylvania. A large circle of stones that appear to emerge from the earth creates a site for contemplation.

The Meeting Room

Lin has gone on to design other open-air spaces for community and contemplation. One such place is "The Meeting Room," built in 2013. Located in Queen Anne Square in Newport, Rhode Island, Lin describes the design of the site as

> ... the creation of stone foundations and rooms that trace the pre-existing building foundations at this site.
>
> Each of the three foundations represents a different century—the eighteenth, nineteenth, and twentieth—and texts from historic documents from those periods have been carved into the thresholds, capturing in subject matter, phrasing, and lettering the voice of each era. The quotes were selected from historic journals, each focused on a different aspect of life, from domesticity and the hearth, to the main industries of sailing and farming, to the builder's trade. [8]

This time Lin combined the landscape of the square with the historical artifacts and documents of the place to allow people today to connect with the residents of the past.

not to do." Basically, he said, Maya Lin "simply cleared a sitting space for openair meditation."[9]

Topo

From the Peace Chapel, Lin went on to another landscape design. In 1990, she travelled to Charlotte, North Carolina, to work on what was called "an environmental art work."[10] The outdoor project was created for the Charlotte Coliseum, a sports stadium. Sponsored by

Lin discussed her redesign of Newport, Rhode Island's Queen Anne Square in 2011. Lin collaborated with landscape artist Edwina von Gal in the art installation located at the park.

the city's planning commission, it was an unusual—and successful—effort to beautify the surroundings of a sports complex.

Lin used giant topiary bushes planted on the long traffic approach to the coliseum to carry out her theme. Topiary landscaping is trimming or shaping trees or shrubbery into ornamental shapes. It is an admired feature of many famous gardens, especially in the southern states.

Lin brought in landscape architect Henry Arnold to work with her. It was he who had designed Constitution Gardens in Washington, DC, the site of the Vietnam Veterans Memorial. He had also advised Lin about the landscape problems connected with that site.

For this project in Charlotte, Lin wanted holly bushes to be trimmed into giant balls to carry out the sports theme of her design. They would, once planted, grow on the sloping plane of ground that slanted down to the coliseum. But finding holly bushes as large as Lin needed was not easy.

A landscape consultant in Charlotte searched the city for them. Finally, he found ten huge holly bushes on the circular drive of an old house. The owner agreed to sell them. Then they were excavated and planted on the site of the coliseum project.

Problems as huge as the holly bushes had to be solved before the specimens were in place. Drainage, grading, retaining walls—all were tackled, with the help of many workmen and heavy machinery. Lin found herself, a lone female, telling a crew of burly laborers what she wanted them to do.[11] She was undaunted, confident, as she said, that women, too, can learn to build things.[12]

A writer who observed the landscape design taking shape described it as "a giant, droll topiary park" with holly bushes appearing "to be rolling downhill one after another."[13] Lin called it "surreal, absolutely fun—a stage set the public can be part of."[14] The people of Charlotte call it "Topo."

The city of Charlotte sold the Coliseum in 2007, and the building was imploded. And with it went Topo. Lin and Arnold's creation was demolished in 2008. Lin did not comment on the situation, but it is likely she felt that its life had run its course.

Storm King Wavefield

Inspired by the earthen burial mounds she saw at the Hopewell and Adena Indian sites she visited in rural Ohio as a child, Lin designed and built a series of three "wavefields," one called "The Wave Field" in Ann

Continuing her focus on nature, Lin designed and built three wavefields, including this one in Michigan. The structures echo both ocean waves and rolling hills.

Arbor, Michigan (1995), another called "Flutter" in Miami, Florida (2005), and the third (and largest) in Mountainville, New York (2009).

Commissioned by the Storm King Art Center, Lin's wavefield comprises seven rows of rolling waves of earth and native grasses over an eleven-acre site that was once a giant gravel pit. The swelling peaks of the waves were inspired by waves but echo the hills and mountains that surround them.

In her autobiographical book *Boundaries*, Lin writes, "My affinity has always been toward sculpting the earth. This impulse has shaped my entire body of work."[15]

Lin repeated this landscape-conscious art style in a 2013 installation called "A Fold in the Field," in New Zealand. Her "largest and most ambitious earthwork to date,"[16] this piece consists of five folds, and is located on Gibbs's Farm, where grazing sheep keep the grass shorn.

"All my artwork has been focused on nature and topography and terrain, and in a way, I'm like a landscape painter," Lin says of her work.[17]

Chapter 10

"**I** used to be terrified that at 21, I might already have outdone myself. Now I'm too busy to think about that,"[1] Maya Lin said back in 1989. Little did Lin know then that she would become one of the most sought-after designers, and that she would go on to win many of the country's top design awards.

Celebrating Women at Yale

In 1990, Yale University's president, Benno Schmidt, asked Lin asked to design a memorial to honor the presence of women in the university. The memorial would come to celebrate the years of the presence of women students at Yale.

It was especially appropriate for one of Yale's most distinguished alumnae to create such a memorial. Yale had been home to Lin as both an undergraduate student and a graduate student, for seven years in all.

The memorial was installed on Cross Campus, Yale's main quadrangle. Located across from the central college library, Cross Campus is where students gather to "hang out and just be part of the campus,"[2] as Lin said.

The memorial is a low, polished green granite oval, set on a stone base, not much over three feet high. As with the Civil Rights Memorial, water flows gently over the oval "table." "Inscribed upon the ellipse is a spiral of numbers that traces the presence of women at the

Dedicated in 1993, Women's Table commemorates the opening of Yale University to women. The sculpture was intended to be a nurturing, communal gathering space in the heart of the campus.

university, counting the number of women enrolled at Yale each year from when they were not accepted (0's) to the present year. The choice of a spiral was made to mark a beginning but to leave the future open, with the last number inscribed marking the number of women enrolled for the year in which the piece was dedicated [1993].[3]

Indoor Art

The Metropolitan Transit Authority of New York City commissioned Lin to create a piece of art for its then-new Penn Station concourse. She designed a futuristic-style clock, fourteen feet wide, to be set into a recess in the vaulted ceiling of the station. Installed in August 1994, "Eclipsed Time" as Maya Lin titled her work, was described by writers as resembling a "gorgeous overhead solar system of a clock."[4] Lights installed behind the conceptual clock indicate the time.

Lin's environmentally inspired studio art has appeared in individual and group museum and gallery exhibitions in the United States and around the world. Recent exhibits include "Tahoe: A Visual History" (2015) at the Nevada Museum of Art, Reno, Nevada; "Rivers and Mountains" (2014) in Ivorypress Space, Madrid, Spain; and "Here and There" (2013) at the Pace Gallery, New York City.

Architectural Commissions

The Museum of African Art in New York City asked Lin to design the interior of the two lower floors of their remodeled building in lower Manhattan. The interior

Lin was photographed during the construction of *2x4 Landscape*. The installation was created from more than fifty thousand 2x4 boards covering 2,400 square feet (223 square meters).

was opened to the public in 1993. *The New York Times* art critic, Herbert Muschamp, wrote that Lin had designed a "flowing sequence of galleries."[5] She used different colors, materials, and lighting as well as curving walls to help the flow from one area to another.

The museum features all aspects of African life and culture, from ritual emblems and altars to sculptures and handicrafts. This was the type of project that Lin especially welcomed. She would design a similar project for the Museum of Chinese in America in lower Manhattan in 2009.

Lin has designed several private homes. "The Box House" in Telluride, Colorado, is four thousand square feet and made of two wood-clad boxes connected by outdoor decks. Set at the edge of an aspen forest, the house provides a panoramic view of its surroundings. A house that she designed in Santa Monica, California, was described as "a vertical, steel and glass house."[6] She also designed an addition to her own family home in Athens, Ohio.

What Is Missing?

A committed environmentalist, Lin is "creating a global memorial to the planet"[7] called "What Is Missing?" The goal of this memorial is to raise awareness about the mass extinction of species caused by a loss of habitat.

The memorial combines site installations, a book, and a regularly updated website that features videos; time lines of the destruction of species as well as conservation efforts; disasters likely to have been caused by human actions; personal memories that visitors to the site can add, and suggestions for what viewers can to do help stop the destruction.

Lin considers this to be her final memorial. "My love as a child was the environment . . . I'm part of what I would say is a groundswell of thought, concerned activity that would help the world change its course."[8]

Awards and Recognition

Lin has received some of the most prestigious design awards for her innovation and excellence, including the Presidential Design Award, National Medal of Arts, and

Maya Lin was not cowed by her early success. She has continued to explore landscape through a balance of art and architecture.

the Award in Architecture from the American Academy of Arts & Letters.

In addition to her honorary doctorate in fine arts from Yale, she has received honorary doctorates from Harvard University, Brown University, Williams College, and Smith College. In 2000, Lin was inducted into the Academy of Achievement. In 2005, she was proud to be inducted into the Women's Hall of Fame.

What's Next?

At the age of only twenty-one, Maya Lin set the bar for achievement incredibly high with what journalist Jill Kirschenbaum called "superb design [that] has changed the way war memorials are perceived."[9] Her early success with the Vietnam Veterans Memorial could have derailed the rest of her career, but Lin refused to let it.

She has since moved from one success to another, from one art form to another, from one medium to another—always looking for that "balance between East and West, actually between sciences and art, between mathematics and artistics."[10] With her ambitious project "What Is Missing?" she is looking to do no less than help save the world as she remains true to her lifelong passion: honoring the environment through her artistic endeavors.

Chronology

1959—On October 5, 1959, Maya Ying Lin was born to Henry Huan Lin and Julia Chang Lin.

1965—1977 Attended public schools in Athens, Ohio.

1977—Graduated from Athens High School.

1977–1981—Attended Yale University.

1981—Announced as the winner of the Vietnam Veterans Memorial design competition.

1981—Graduated from Yale with a bachelor of arts degree.

1981—1982 Worked as a design consultant with an architectural firm in Washington, DC.

1982—Left Washington for Harvard University, where she enrolled in the Graduate School of Design.

1983—Returned to Yale University as a graduate student in architecture.

1983—1985 Worked on various architectural projects.

1986—Received master's degree in architecture from Yale.

1987—Was awarded honorary doctor of fine arts degree from Yale.

1988—Received Presidential Design Award for the Vietnam Veterans Memorial.

1988—Began work on the Civil Rights Memorial for the Southern Poverty Law Center in Montgomery, Alabama.

1989—Attended dedication of the Civil Rights Memorial.

1989—Designed a topiary landscape project for the Charlotte, North Carolina, Coliseum.

1989—Designed the outdoor Peace Chapel for Juniata College in Huntingdon, Pennsylvania.

1990—Was awarded a grant from the National Endowment for the Arts.

1991—Designed the "Women's Table" at Yale University as a memorial honoring women students at Yale.

1993—Designed the interior of the lower two floors of Museum of African Art in New York City.

1994—Designed "Eclipsed Time," a ceiling clock for Penn Station concourse in New York City.

1995—Designed "The Wave Field" in Ann Arbor, Michigan.

2000—Inducted into the Academy of Achievement.

2005—Designed "Flutter" in Miami, Florida.

2005—Inducted into the Women's Hall of Fame.

2005—First of six installations of "The Confluence Project."

2009—Designed the interior of the Museum of Chinese in America in New York City.

2009—Designed "Storm King Wavefield" in Mountainville, New York.

2009—Launched first installation of last memorial "What Is Missing?"

2013—Designed "A Fold in the Field" in New Zealand.

2013—Designed "The Meeting Room" an outdoor community space in Newport, Rhode Island.

2015—Work featured in various art exhibits around the United States.

2016—Sixth and final installation of "The Confluence Project."

Chapter Notes

CHAPTER 1. DEFINING MOMENTS

1. PBS: Art21 (Art in the Twenty First Century), "SEGMENT:L Maya Lin in 'Identity,'" [15:05], (2001): accessed December 19, 2015, http://www.pbs.org/art21/watch-now/segment-maya-lin-in-identity.

2. *Maya Lin: A Strong, Clear Vision Documentary*, directed by Frida Lee Mock (Ocean Releasing, 2005), DVD.

3. United Press International, "Student Wins War Memorial Contest," *New York Times*, May 7, 1981, http://www.nytimes.com/1981/05/07/us/student-wins-war-memorial-contest.html.

4. Christopher Buckley, "The Wall," *Esquire*, September 1985, p. 66.

5. Jan C. Scruggs and Joel L. Swerdlow, *To Heal a Nation: The Vietnam Veterans Memorial* (New York: Harper and Row, 1985), p. 64.

6. Wolf Von Eckardt, "The Making of a Monument," *Washington Post*, April 26, 1980, https://www.washingtonpost.com/archive/lifestyle/1980/04/26/the-making-of-a-monument/c8d2b13a-d87b-4a29-bf89-a4dc28de2a77/.

7. Joel L. Swerdlow, "To Heal a Nation," adapted from the book by Jan C. Scruggs and Joel L. Swerdlow, *National Geographic*, May 1985, p. 566.

8. United Press International.

9. B. Drummond Ayres Jr., "A Yale Senior, A Vietnam Memorial and a Few Ironies," *New York Times*, June 29, 1981, http://www.nytimes.com/1981/06/29/style

/yale-senior-a-vietnam-memorial-and-a-few-ironies.
html.

10. Benjamin Forgey, "The Statue and the Wall,"
    Washington Post, November 10, 1984, p. D1.

11. Alan Borg, *War Memorials from Antiquity to the
    Present* (London: Cooper, 1991), p. 74.

12. Henry Allen, "Epitaph for Vietnam," *Washington Post*,
    May 7, 1981, https://www.washingtonpost.com
    /archive/lifestyle/1981/05/07/epitaph-for-vietnam
    /b238e59c-7eb8-4f3e-9daa-2590de49c8fb/.

13. AOL-HuffPost Lifestyle (Makers: Women Who Make
    America). "Makers Profile: Maya Lin: Artist, Architect
    & Memorial Designer," [1:36], accessed December 19,
    2015, www.makers.com/maya-lin.

CHAPTER 2. ROOTS IN CHINA

1. Phil McCombs, "Maya Lin and the Great Call of
   China," *Washington Post*, January 3, 1982, https://
   www.washingtonpost.com/archive
   /lifestyle/1982/01/03/maya-lin-and-the-great-call-of-
   china/544d8f2b-43b4-45ec-989b-72b2f2865eb4/.

2. Ibid.

3. "Julia Lin," *The Athens Messenger* (2013): accessed
   December 19, 2015, http://www.athensmessenger
   .com/obituaries/julia-lin/article_436f09b3-2511-5530-
   bd46-4f14bf43d447.html.

4. McCombs.

5. SinoVision English Channel Archives, "Maya Lin,"
   YouTube video, [9:22], (2012): accessed December 19,
   2015, www.youtube.com/watch?v=vLyXqY0X2iE.

6. McCombs.

7. SinoVision English Channel Archives. [1:52].

8. McCombs.

9. SinoVision English Channel Archives. [7:42].

10. Maya Lin, "Museum of Chinese in America," Maya Lin Studio, Accessed December 19, 2015, www.mayalin.com.

11. SinoVision English Channel Archives. [10:32].

12. Carol Kramer, "The Wall: Monument to a Nation's Sacrifice," *McCall's*, June 1988, pp. 42–45.

13. McCombs.

14. Jonathan Coleman, "First She Looks Inward: Maya Lin," *Time*, November 26, 1989, http://content.time.com/time/magazine/article/0,9171,958945,00.html.

15. McCombs.

16. Coleman.

17. Brent Ashabranner, *Always to Remember: The Story of the Vietnam Veterans Memorial* (New York: Putnam, 1988), p. 39.

18. Maya Lin, letter to author (January 1993).

CHAPTER 3. LIFE AT YALE

1. Phil McCombs, "Maya Lin and the Great Call of China," *Washington Post*, January 3, 1982, https://www.washingtonpost.com/archive/lifestyle/1982/01/03/maya-lin-and-the-great-call-of-china/544d8f2b-43b4-45ec-989b-72b2f2865eb4/.

2. Peter Tauber, "Monument Maker," *New York Times Magazine*, February 24, 1991, http://www.nytimes.com/1991/02/24/magazine/monument-maker.html?pagewanted=all.

3. McCombs.

4. B. Drummond Ayres Jr., "A Yale Senior, a Vietnam Memorial and a Few Ironies," *New York Times*, June 29, 1981, http://www.nytimes.com/1981/06/29/style /yale-senior-a-vietnam-memorial-and-a-few-ironies .html.

5. McCombs.

6. Ibid.

7. Ayres.

8. McCombs.

9. PBS: Art21 (Art in the Twenty First Century), "SEGMENT:L Maya Lin in 'Identity,'" [10:34], (2001): accessed December 19, 2015, http://www.pbs.org /art21/watch-now/segment-maya-lin-in-identity.

10. Jonathan Coleman, "First She Looks Inward," *Time*, November 26, 1989, http://content.time.com/time /magazine/article/0,9171,958945,00.html.

11. Lilly Wei, "Maya Lin Interview," *Art in America*, September 1991, p. 128.

12. English Channel Archives, "Maya Lin," *YouTube* video, [2:37], (2012): accessed December 19, 2015, www.youtube.com/watch?v=vLyXqY0X2iE.

CHAPER 4. AN UNLIKELY SELECTION

1. Jan C. Scruggs and Joel L. Swerdlow, *To Heal a Nation: The Vietnam Veterans Memorial* (New York: Harper and Row, 1985), pp. 7–8.

2. Arthur C. Danto, "The Vietnam Veterans Memorial," *The Nation*, August 31, 1985, p. 154.

3. Wolf Von Eckardt, "The Making of a Memorial," *Washington Post*, April 26, 1980, https://www .washingtonpost.com/archive/lifestyle/1980/04/26

the-making-of-a-monument/c8d2b13a-d87b-4a29-bf89-a4dc28de2a77/.

4. Scruggs and Swerdlow, p. 58.

5. Ibid.

6. B. Drummond Ayres Jr., "A Yale Senior, A Vietnam Memorial and a Few Ironies," *New York Times*, June 29, 1981, http://www.nytimes.com/1981/06/29/style /yale-senior-a-vietnam-memorial-and-a-few-ironies .html.

7. Ibid.

8. Joel L. Swerdlow, "To Heal a Nation," adapted from the book by Jan C. Scruggs and Joel L. Swerdlow, *National Geographic*, May 1985, p. 557.

9. Edward Clinton Ezell, Reflections on the Wall: The Vietnam Memorial (Harrisburg, Penn.: Stackpole Books, 1987), p. 16.

10. Phil McCombs, "Maya Lin and the Great Call of China," *Washington Post*, (1982): accessed December 19, 2015.

11. Wolf Von Eckardt, "Of Heart and Mind," *Washington Post*, May 16, 1981, https://www.washingtonpost.com /archive/lifestyle/1981/05/16/of-heart-38/c047f375-a55f-46d5-99c2-8442e5208a71/.

12. "Vietnam Memorial Architect Presents Keynote Address," Bulletin Juniata College Alumni, November 1989, p. 14.

13. Maya Lin, "Interview," *National Geographic*, May 1985, p. 557.

14. Maya Lin, "Letter to the Editor," *New York Times*, July 14, 1981, p. 24.

15. Henry Allen, "Epitaph for Vietnam," *Washington Post*, May 7, 1981, https://www.washingtonpost.com /archive/lifestyle/1981/05/07/epitaph-for-vietnam /b238e59c-7eb8-4f3e-9daa-2590de49c8fb/.

16. Maya Lin, "Interview," *National Geographic*, May 1985, p. 557.

17. Scruggs and Swerdlow, pp. 66–67.

18. Ibid.

19. Maya Lin, letter to author (January 1993).

CHAPTER 5. CONTROVERSY ENSUES

1. Jan C. Scruggs and Joel L. Swerdlow, *To Heal a Nation: The Vietnam Veterans Memorial* (New York: Harper and Row, 1985), p. 79.

2. Elizabeth Hess, "A Tale of Two Memorials," *Art in America*, April 1983, p. 122.

3. Jonathan Coleman, "First She Looks Inward: Maya Lin," *Time*, November 26, 1989, http://content.time .com/time/magazine/article/0,9171,958945,00.html.

4. Ibid.

5. Michael J. Weiss, "The Vietnam War Dead Raises Hope—and Anger," *People Weekly*, March 8, 1982, http://www.people.com/people/archive /article/0,,20081603,00.html.

6. Coleman.

7. Phil McCombs, "Maya Lin and the Great Call of China," *The Washington Post*, January 3, 1982, https:// www.washingtonpost.com/archive /lifestyle/1982/01/03/maya-lin-and-the-great-call-of- china/544d8f2b-43b4-45ec-989b-72b2f2865eb4/.

8. Ibid.

9. Scruggs and Swerdlow, p. 56.

10. Joel L. Swerdlow, "To Heal a Nation," adapted from the book by Jan C. Scruggs and Joel L. Swerdlow, *National Geographic*, May 1985, p. 557.

11. Hess, pp. 125–126.

12. Wolf Von Eckhardt, "Storm over a Vietnam Memorial," *Time*, November 9, 1981, p. 103.

13. Maya Lin, "Making the Memorial," *NYBooks.com* (2000): accessed December 19, 2015, www.nybooks .com/articles/2000/11/02/making-the-memorial.

14. Weiss.

15. AOL-HuffPost Lifestyle (Makers: Women Who Make America), "Makers Profile: Maya Lin: Artist, Architect & Memorial Designer," [2:02], accessed December 19, 2015, www.makers.com/maya-lin.

16. Benjamin Forgey, "The Statue and the Wall," *Washington Post*, November 10, 1984, p. D8.

17. Scruggs and Swerdlow, p. 56.

18. Ibid.

19. B. Drummond Ayres Jr., "A Yale Senior, a Vietnam Memorial and a Few Ironies," *New York Times*, June 29, 1981, http://www.nytimes.com/1981/06/29/style /yale-senior-a-vietnam-memorial-and-a-few-ironies .html.

20. Scruggs and Swerdlow, p. 64.

21. Ibid.

22. Elizabeth Kastor, "Maya Lin's Unwavering Vision," *Washington Post*, February 13, 1989, p. B6.

23. Wolf Von Eckardt, "Of Heart and Mind," *Washington Post*, May 16, 1981, https://www.washingtonpost.com

/archive/lifestyle/1981/05/16/of-heart-38/c047f375-a55f-46d5-99c2-8442e5208a71/.

24. Ibid.

25. Washington Diarist, "Downcast Eyes," *New Republic*, November 28, 1982, p. 42.

26. Hess, p. 122.

27. Isabel Wilkerson, "Art War Erupts over Vietnam Veterans Memorial," *Washington Post,* July 8, 1982, p. D3.

28. Scruggs and Swerdlow, p. 101.

CHAPTER 6. BUILDING THE MEMORIAL

1. Maya Lin. "Making the Memorial," *NYBooks.com* (2000): accessed December 20, 2015, www.nybooks.com/articles/2000/11/02/making-the-memorial.

2. Ibid.

3. Elizabeth Kastor, "Maya Lin's Unwavering Vision," *Washington Post*, February 3, 1989, https://www.washingtonpost.com/archive/lifestyle/1989/02/13/maya-lins-unwavering-vision/0dadb59c-2a1c-4ed1-b321-c937d3f64a72/.

4. Weis.

5. Brent Ashabranner, *Always to Remember: The Story of the Vietnam Veterans Memorial* (New York: Putnam, 1988), p. 92.

6. Lilly Wei, "Maya Lin Interview," *Art in America*, September 1991, pp. 127–128.

7. Peter Tauber, "Monument Maker," *New York Times Magazine*, February 24, 1991,http://www.nytimes.com/1991/02/24/magazine/monument-maker.html?pagewanted=all.

8. Maya Lin, "Making the Memorial," *NYBooks.com* (2000): accessed December 20, 2015, www.nybooks .com/articles/2000/11/02/making-the-memorial.

9. Ashabranner, p. 55.

10. "Model of Civil Rights Memorial Unveiled," *New York Times*, July 30, 1988, http://www.nytimes .com/1988/07/30/us/model-of-civil-rights-memorial- unveiled.html.

11. Joel L. Swerdlow, "To Heal a Nation," adapted from the book by Jan C. Scruggs and Joel L. Swerdlow, *National Geographic*, May 1985, p. 557.

12. Ibid., p. 572.

13. Elizabeth Hess, "A Tale of Two Memorials," *Art in America*, April 1983, p. 126.

14. Arthur C. Danto, "The Vietnam Veterans Memorial," *The Nation*, August 31, 1985, p. 154.

CHAPTER 7. MOVING ON FROM THE WALL

1. Maggie Malone, "Up Against the Wall," *Newsweek*, January 20, 1986, p. 6.

2. Jonathan Coleman, "First She Looks Inward," *Time*, November 1989, http://content.time.com/time /magazine/article/0,9171,958945,00.html.

3. Malone, p. 6.

4. Phil McCombs, "Maya Lin and the Great Call of China," *Washington Post*, January 3, 1982, https:// www.washingtonpost.com/archive /lifestyle/1982/01/03/maya-lin-and-the-great-call-of- china/544d8f2b-43b4-45ec-989b-72b2f2865eb4/.

5. Benjamin Forgey, "The Statue and the Wall," *Washington Post*, November 10, 1984, p. D8.

6. James M. Mayo, *War Memorials as Political Landscape* (New York: Praeger, 1988), p. 205.

7. Forgey, p. D8.

8. Maya Lin, "Beauty and the Bank," *New Republic*, December 23, 1985, pp. 25–29.

9. Ibid.

10. Elizabeth Kastor, "Maya Lin's Unwavering Vision," *Washington Post*, February 3, 1989, https://www
.washingtonpost.com/archive/lifestyle/1989/02/13
/maya-lins-unwavering-vision/0dadb59c-2a1c-4ed1-
b321-c937d3f64a72/.

11. Peter Tauber, "Monument Maker," *New York Times Magazine*, February 24, 1991, http://www.nytimes
.com/1991/02/24/magazine/monument-maker
.html?pagewanted=all.

12. Kastor.

13. Jill Kirschenbaum, "The Symmetry of Maya Lin," *Ms.*, September/October 1990, pp. 20–21.

14. Ibid.

15. Tauber, p. 50.

16. Benjamin Forgey, "Commission Vetoes Vietnam Women's Statue," *Washington Post*, October 23, 1987, p. B1.

17. Ibid.

18. Benjamin Forgey, "Women and the Wall," *Washington Post*, October 22, 1987, p. E1.

19. Editorial, *Washington Post*, November 11, 1987, p. A22.

20. Karen Swisher, "Maya Lin's Memorial Defense," *Washington Post*, February 24, 1988, https://www
.washingtonpost.com/archive/lifestyle/1988/02/24

/maya-lins-memorial-defense/5e775b5c-3684-43ec-83c6-1bdd6d2f06ee/.

21. "A Legacy of Healing and Hope," *Vietnam Women's Memorial Project Inc.* (Washington, D.C., February/March 1993).

22. Ibid.

23. Laura Palmer, "How to Bandage a War," *New York Times Magazine*, November 7, 1993, p. 8.

CHAPTER 8. A SECOND MEMORIAL

1. Jonathan Coleman, "First She Looks Inward," *Time*, November 26, 1989, http://content.time.com/time/magazine/article/0,9171,958945,00.html.

2. Maya Lin, "Making the Memorial," *NYBooks.com* (2000): accessed December 20, 2015, www.nybooks.com/articles/2000/11/02/making-the-memorial.

3. Charles Gandee, "Gandee at Large," *House and Garden*, March 1990, p. 214.

4. Peter Tauber, "Monument Maker," *New York Times Magazine*, February 24, 1991, http://www.nytimes.com/1991/02/24/magazine/monument-maker.html?pagewanted=all.

5. William Zinsser, "I Realized Her Tears Were Becoming Part of the Memorial,," *Smithsonian*, September 1991, p. 36.

6. Southern Poverty Law Center, *Free at Last: A History of the Civil Rights Movement and Those Who Died in the Struggle* (Montgomery, Alabama: Southern Poverty Law Center, 1989), p. 104.

7. Jill Kirschenbaum, "The Symmetry of Maya Lin," *Ms.*, September/October 1990, p. 22.

8. Zinssner, p. 36.

9. Coleman, p. 94.

10. Zinsser, p. 39.

11. Elizabeth Kastor, "Maya Lin's Unwavering Vision," *Washington Post*, February 12, 1989, https://www.washingtonpost.com/archive/lifestyle/1989/02/13/maya-lins-unwavering-vision/0dadb59c-2a1c-4ed1-b321-c937d3f64a72/.

12. Kastor, p. B6.

13. Kate Christensen, "A Civilized Memorial," *Seventeen*, June 1990, p. 40.

14. Zinsser, p. 35.

15. Ibid.

16. David Grogan, "Maya Lin Lets Healing Waters Flow over Her Civil Rights Memorial," *People Weekly*, November 20, 1989, http://www.people.com/people/archive/article/0,,20115985,00.html.

17. Gandee, p. 214.

18. Kastor, p. B6.

CHAPTER 9. LANDSCAPE PAINTER

1. PBS: Art21 (Art in the Twenty First Century), "SEGMENT:L Maya Lin in 'Identity,'" [16:30] (2001): accessed December 20, 2015, http://www.pbs.org/art21/watch-now/segment-maya-lin-in-identity.

2. "Vietnam Memorial Architect Presents Keynote Address," Bulletin Juniata College Alumni, November 1989, p. 14.

3. Ibid.

4. Ibid.

5. Maya Lin, "Remarks at Peace Chapel Dedication," *Juniata College*, October 14, 1989, p. 1.

6. Ibid.

7. Ibid.

8. Maya Lin. "The Meeting Room, Queen Anne Square, Newport, Rhode Island, 2013," accessed December 20, 2015, mayalin.com.

9. Peter Tauber, "Monument Maker," *New York Times Magazine*, February 24, 1991, http://www.nytimes.com/1991/02/24/magazine/monument-maker.html?pagewanted=all.

10. Ibid.

11. Ibid.

12. Lilly Wei, "Maya Lin Interview," *Art in America*, September 1991, p. 128.

13. Tauber, p. 52.

14. Ibid.

15. Maya Lin, "A Fold in the Field, 2013," accessed December 20, 2015, mayalin.com.

16. Maya Lin, *Boundaries*, (New York: Simon & Schuster, 2006), p. 7:03.

17. SinoVision English Channel Archives, "Maya Lin," *YouTube* video, [5:07], (2012): accessed December 19, 2015, www.youtube.com/watch?v=vLyXqY0X2iE.

CHAPTER 10. A MOMENT'S INSPIRATION

1. Maggie Malone, "Up Against the Wall," *Newsweek*, January 20, 1986, p. 6.

2. Diana West, "A Monument of One's Own," *The American Spectator*, May 1992, p. 58.

3. Maya Lin, "The Women's Table," accessed December 20, 2015, mayalin.com.

4. Peter Plagens and Yahlin Chang, "Maya Lin's Time for Light," *Newsweek*, August 8, 1994, p. 52.

5. Herbert Muschamp, "Crossing Cultural Boundaries," *New York Times*, February 12, 1993, p. C1.

6. Charles Gandee, "People Are Talking About Maya Lin," *Vogue*, February 1993, p. 61.

7. "What Is Missing?" accessed December 20, 2015, whatismissing.net/#info/menu.

8. "Maya Lin: What is Missing?," [1:32] (2014): accessed December 20, 2015, www.youtube.com /watch?v=cx2zlvpM_Ag.

9. Jill Kirschenbaum, "The Symmetry of Maya Lin," *Ms.*, September/October 1990, p. 20.

10. SinoVision English Channel Archives, "Maya Lin," *YouTube* video, [0:13], (2012): accessed December 19, 2015, www.youtube.com/watch?v=vLyXqY0X2iE.

Glossary

apprentice—One person who works for another to learn a trade.

architecture—The profession of designing artificial constructions such as buildings, open areas, and environments, usually with some consideration for aesthetic effect.

ceramics—The art of making objects from clay and other materials treated by baking in extremely high heat.

commission—To place an order for something.

controversy—A long public debate or dispute concerning a matter of opinion.

design—A preliminary sketch or plan for a work to be executed.

draft—The compulsory enrollment of people for military service.

draft evader—A person who avoids the compulsory enrollment for military service, often by moving to another country.

earthwork—Maya Lin's term for large-scale art installations involving a shaping of the terrain.

environmentalist—An advocate for the protection of Earth and its inhabitants.

fund drive—The organized act of asking for money to reach a stated goal.

honorary degree—A academic degree for which the university has waived the typical requirements.

infantryman—A soldier.

installation—A type of art that is usually three-dimensional, chosen for a particular site, and intended to change the perception of a place.

landscape designer—A person trained in the art of combining nature and culture.

memorial—Something designed and established to remind people of an event, person, or people.

modern art—Art that emphasizes individual experimentation.

sculpture—The art of making two- or three-dimensional forms that are representational or abstract.

studio art—Artwork that is created in the workplace of the artist.

Further Reading

Books

Doubek, Robert W. *Creating the Vietnam Veterans Memorial: The Inside Story*. Jefferson, North Carolina: McFarland & Company, 2015

Lin, Maya. *Boundaries*. New York: Simon & Schuster, 2006.

Lin, Maya. *Here and There*. New York: PaceWildenstein, 2013.

Lin, Maya, Michael Brensin, William L. Fox, Paul Goldberger, and John McPhee. *Topologies*. New York, Rizzoli, 2015.

Scruggs, Jan C., and Joel L. Swerdlow, *To Heal a Nation: The Vietnam Veterans Memorial*. New York: Harper and Row, 1985.

Websites

Maya Lin Studios
mayalin.com
Showcase of Maya Lin's art installations, architecture projects, and memorials, each accompanied by a description written by the artist.

Maya Lin
pbs.org/art21/artists/maya-lin
Brief biography and collection of video interviews with the artist.

Maya Lin: Artist, Architect & Memorial Designer
makers.com/maya-lin
Brief biography and a short interview of the artist.

Film
Maya Lin: A Strong Clear Vision. Directed by Frieda Lee Mock. 2003.

Index